The
Golden Crucible

AN INTRODUCTION TO THE HISTORY
OF AMERICAN CALIFORNIA: 1850-1905

BY

BLAKE ROSS

FIRST PRIZE ESSAY
JAMES D. PHELAN HISTORICAL ESSAY
CONTEST

Held under the auspices of the San Francisco Branch,
League of American Pen Women

SAN FRANCISCO
PAUL ELDER AND COMPANY
PUBLISHERS
1930

SECOND PRINTING

TABLE OF CONTENTS

Introduction
    By the Honorable James D. Phelan   VII

Judging the Ten Best Essays
    By Judge John F. Davis   IX

Letter of Award
    By Professor Sidney Edward Mezes   XVI

Letter of Appreciation
    By Carl I. Wheat   XVII

Appreciation
    By Robert E. Cowan   XVIII

Criticism
    By Oscar Lewis   XIX

Preface
    By B. R.   XX

Foreword
    By Mrs. Frederick H. Colburn   XXI

The Golden Crucible
    By B. R.   3

Addenda
    Social and Intellectual Life of California   87

Acknowledgment
    And Bibliography   97

{v}

INTRODUCTION

BY THE HONORABLE JAMES D. PHELAN

"The Golden Crucible" is well named, because, first of all, in the minds of the people, California is regarded as the Golden State. It was not the actual discovery by Cabrillo that awakened wonder, but the discovery of gold by Marshall. The heroic days were the days of the vast immigration following the uncovering of the precious metal.

It is a sad commentary on the historic priorities and proprieties that the Legislature, in selecting two men to grace the Hall of Fame, in Washington, omitted to select anyone associated with the Golden Age.

An essay necessarily is concise and compact and Blake Ross has put into his story only the essential things. He has amalgamated the grains of fact into a nugget of truth. His achievement may well give promise of another work, fuller and more comprehensive, which will allot to each passing phase of California life its appropriate place, and do justice to the great men who laid the foundation of the State.

JUDGING THE TEN BEST ESSAYS
BY JUDGE JOHN F. DAVIS
Chairman of Local Judging Committee

As stated by Mrs. Frederick H. Colburn, the Chairman of this Prize Historical Essay Contest, in her clearly written Foreword, the official printed announcement therein quoted by her, was, together with the original copies of the fifty-eight essays therein referred to, delivered to myself as Chairman of the Local Judging Committee. The essays were numbered, 1 to 58, inclusive, and the name of each essay placed opposite its number, but no trace whatever given of each author's name or residence,—that information being in her breast, and on a list contained in a safe deposit box in San Francisco, of which she alone had the key, and the names or residences of the writers of each of those 58 essays being given to the Local Judging Committee only after the ten best had been ascertained by the Local Judging Committee.

The Local Judging Committee met at my office in the Humboldt Bank Building, organized, and worked faithfully at the winnowing out of the essays of lesser quality. It was a long and tedious job, but we finally arrived at a unanimous decision, and thereupon notified the Chairman of the Commission as follows:

"San Francisco, Calif.

"Mrs. F. H. Colburn,
President, San Francisco League of American
    Penwomen,
757 Sutter Street,
San Francisco, California.
"Dear Mrs. Colburn:
    "We, the undersigned, being the members of the committee named in the Honorable James D. Phelan Essay Contest in the official announcement, a printed copy of which is hereunto attached and made a part hereof, hereby report that from the fifty-eight essays submitted by you to us, we have selected the following ten, to-wit: numbers 3, 8, 19, 21, 28, 38, 43, 46, 51 and 52 as the best ten of those submitted, and we have forwarded them to Professor Sidney Mezes of the University of New York City, New York, by

American Railway Express, together with a duplicate printed copy of the official announcement hereunto attached, and a letter, of which we enclose you a carbon copy, for the selection by him therefrom of two essays, pursuant to the conditions set forth in said official announcement.

"The remaining forty-eight essays not forwarded to Professor Mezes are hereby returned to you, in order that you may return them to the parties, respectively, from whom you received the same.

"Dated January 23, 1929.

"Respectfully submitted,

JOHN F. DAVIS, Chairman,
HENRY MEADE BLAND,
HERBERT E. BOLTON,
CHARLES S. CUSHING,
BOUTWELL DUNLAP."

The reason why the names and residences of the writers of each of the non-winning 48 of these 58 essays were so disclosed at this time was, that they might be delivered back to Mrs. Colburn, so that she might return them to the respective writers with the announcement that they had not been successful in becoming writers of any of the first ten essays, and to avoid unnecessary strain of waiting, as long as the Local Judging Committees had no further jurisdiction of these particular 48 essays.

The ten best essays (all matters before the Local Judging Committee being settled by numbers alone and without any other possible information) were then forwarded to Professor Sidney E. Mezes, together with full instructions of the terms of the contest, in order that he might make the award to the Local Judging Committee of the first and second best of these ten, designating such awards as first and second prize, by their respective numbers (for he had no more information as to authorship or names or addresses than the Local Judging Committee).

Then came the most remarkable set of coincidences which illustrates the difference in time that it takes to find a person by the transmission of a package in this country as compared with the method adopted on the Continent of Europe, even by American Companies operating there, for the length of time it took, not so much to ascertain the whereabouts of Professor Mezes but to have the package forwarded to him, was maddening.

In the first place, he had been away on the Continent on a two years' vacation from the University of New York City for his health and none of us had known anything about it.

As soon as the Committee had decided upon the ten best essays, they were forwarded to Professor Mezes through the American Express Company here, accompanied by a letter of the full Committee, on January 23, 1929, addressed to:

"Professor Sidney Mezes,
University of New York City,
New York City, N. Y.
"Dear Professor Mezes:
"We, the undersigned, being the committee of the Honorable James D. Phelan Prize Contest of Historical Essays on the History of California from 1850 to 1905, named in the official announcement of said contest, a printed original of which is hereunto attached and made a part hereof, have forwarded to you under separate cover, by American Express, essays numbered, respectively, 3, 8, 19, 21, 28, 38, 43, 46, 51 and 52 as being the best ten essays of those submitted to us in order that you may, pursuant to the provisions of the printed announcement, make selection of the two best essays of said ten for the first and second prize, respectively, set forth in said announcement.

"The names and addresses of the writers are known only to Mrs. F. H. Colburn, President, San Francisco League of American Pen Women, 757 Sutter Street, San Francisco, California, who will disclose the same to you as soon as you have finished your examination and made your decision.

"Dated, January 23, 1929.
        "Respectfully submitted,
                JOHN F. DAVIS, Chairman,
                HENRY MEADE BLAND,
                HERBERT E. BOLTON,
                CHARLES S. CUSHING,
                BOUTWELL DUNLAP."

In reply thereto I received the following telegram:

New York City, Jan. 31, 1929.

"John F. Davis,
1404 Humboldt Bank Bldg.
San Francisco, California.

"Letter to Dr. Sidney E. Mezes received. Dr. Mezes residing in Europe for two years. Stop. American Express is holding insured package awaiting your instructions. Stop. Address of Dr. Mezes is care of Guaranty Trust Company, 3, Rue des Italiens, Paris, France. Do you wish me to forward your letter to him?

"H. L. McCARTIE,
College of the City of New York,"

to which I immediately answered by nightletter on February 2, 1929:

"H. L. McCartie,
College of the City of New York,
New York City, N. Y.

"Your telegram thirty-first January received. Kindly forward my letter to him. Stop. Kindly also instruct American Express to forward to Dr. Mezes insured package letting me know cost of expressage or you pay it and I will remit cost to you.

"JOHN F. DAVIS,
1404 Humboldt Bank Bldg., San Francisco, Calif."

In reply to this urgent nightletter of February 2nd, 1929, I received from Professor McCartie the following letter:

"I am sending on your letter to Dr. Mezes, but am informed by the American Express (the agency through which I forwarded the essays) that you will have to send directions to them personally regarding the insured package. They advise me that you are to write Dr. S. J. Schofield, Agent Onhand Department, American Railway Express, 438 West 55th St., New York, N. Y., and instruct him to where the package is to be addressed. Dr. Mezes address in Europe is care of Guaranty Trust Company, 3, Rue des Italiens, Paris, France," the letter being written on the letterhead of the office of the President of the College of the City of New York.

To this, I answered, as soon as received at San Francisco, February 8, 1929:

"H. L. McCartie, Esq.,
Office of the President,
College of the City of New York,
Convent Ave. and 139th St.,
New York, N. Y.

"Dear Sir:

"Thank you very much for yours of the 4th inst., which I have just received.

"On the suggestion of the American Express Company stated in your letter, I have just sent them instructions to the address given in your letter as to the forwarding of the package to Dr. Mezes.

"Thanking you for your great courtesy in letting me know what to do in the premises, I am,

"Very sincerely,
"JOHN F. DAVIS."

Having received this letter from Professor McCartie and not yet having received any letter from Professor Mezes to my letter direct to him on January 23, 1929, and having received supplementary instructions from the offices of the Guaranty Trust Company referring me back to the local agents here of the American Express Company as to the proper forwarding of the package, and being now informed of the true address of Dr. Mezes in Europe and not yet having received any answer from him to my letter to him of the previous month from San Francisco, I thereupon followed up the correspondence that I had had with Mr. McCartie, the American Express Company in Paris and the local agents of the American Express Company in San Francisco and sent a direct letter to Dr. Sidney Mezes at the address now given me by all the powers that be as being the correct one and as destined to discover the two-year traveler somewhere, I wrote Dr. Sidney Mezes as follows:

"Dr. Sidney Mezes,
c/o Guaranty Trust Company,
3, Rue des Italiens,
Paris, France.

"My dear Professor Mezes:

"Referring to the letter to you from San Francisco, dated January 23, 1929, and signed by the Committee headed by myself as Chairman, sending you ten Essays in the James D. Phelan Prize Contest of Historical Essays from which you were to pick two as the best, I have to advise that said Essays were sent by the American Railway Express to you at the College of the City of New York, New York.

"I have been advised by Professor H. L. McCartie, of the College of the City of New York, that you have been residing in Europe for two years and that the American Railway Express is holding the package awaiting further instructions, also informing me that your address is c/o Guaranty Trust Company, 3, Rue des Italiens, Paris France, and I suppose he has forwarded my letter to you.

"In the meantime, I am advised by the Express Company from New York that the package is at *their* office there and asking my further instructions. I have today gotten in touch with the local office of the American Railway Express *at 2nd and Mission Streets here,* and, upon the suggestion of the chief clerk, before advising the *New York office of the American Railway Express Company to forward the package beyond New York,* I am now writing *to you to ask you* to what address in Europe it would be agreeable to you to have the same forwarded, or if perchance you might be coming to New York. The idea is *not to have the package pass you on the way* in case you are due to return at this time, and if you are not due to return at this time, to get the specific address in Europe to which the same should be forwarded, instead of forwarding it to Paris and possibly having some complications about having it forwarded further in Europe from there.

"Upon receipt of Prof. H. L. McCartie's telegram, I, on the 2nd inst., wired him to forward your letter, so I suppose you have received that letter by this time. My first instruction was to forward the package immediately, but upon the notice from the New York Express Company office, I took the matter up with the local office here and that is why I felt it necessary to send this supplemental letter, *so as to make assurance doubly sure.*

"Thanking you in advance for the courtesy of a reply, I am,

"With best wishes,

"Very sincerely,

"JOHN F. DAVIS."

And finally came upon the trail of the wanderer in the little note attached to this particular letter and returned to me, as follows:

"John F. Davis, Esq.,

Dear Sir:

"Please excuse this informality, but I am barely up from the grippe and every little extra is a burden.

"I expect to be in Europe *for all of '29, so please send the essays in care Guaranty Trust Co., rue des Italiens, Paris;* they will forward. If they could reach me by April 15th, or a little after, it would be helpful, as soon after that I get on the move. *I shall act promptly.*

"Thanking you for your trouble,

"Sincerely yours,

"S. E. MEZES."

Then finally came the Letter of Award, dated May 2nd, 1929, from Prof. Sidney Edward Mezes to the Local Judging Committee, set out in full on the following page.

Mrs. Frederick H. Colburn, upon the publication of Professor Mezes' award, immediately carried out in all fidelity every remaining detail of the work which has been a long labor of love for everybody connected with it from the gentleman who furnished the money for the prizes to the dotting of the last i and the crossing of the last t.

LETTER OF AWARD

BY PROFESSOR SIDNEY EDWARD MEZES
President of the University of the City of New York

Grasse, France, May 2, 1929.

Honorable John F. Davis, chairman, and Messrs.
Henry Meade Bland, Herbert E. Bolton, Charles
S. Cushing and Boutwell Dunlap.

Dear Sirs:

I beg to acknowledge receipt of essays 3, 8, 19, 21,
28, 38, 43, 46, 51 and 52, sent me by you as the duly
authorized committee, as the best ten essays of those submitted to you, in the Honorable James D. Phelan Prize
Contest of Historical Essays on the History of California
from 1850 to 1905; and to advise you that, according to
the conditions of the contest, and under the duty imposed
upon me, I have selected as the best essay No. 46, and
for the second prize No. 19.

No. 46 seems to me to stand out for its strong simple
English and for a style that leads one on; and to excel
in its grasp of the essence of the period and in the mar-
shalling of its facts into one coherent history, without,
I think, doing any violence to reality. It is not as rich in
detail as some other essays, but its qualities seem to me
to overtop this defect.

No. 19, by contrast, is full of fact and episodic, at
some sacrifice, it may be, of wholeness, of a view of the
essence of the period. But the episodes are well told, and
the mosaic as a whole presents an interesting and comprehensive picture of times as unique as they were significant. Thus the two essays are happily complementary.

Please present my remembrances and regards to Senator
Phelan, and my congratulations on the valuable outcome
of his fine enterprise. It must have done much to awaken
a widespread interest in the arresting history of our splendid State and I feel it to have been a privilege, as it was
a pleasure, to have had a part in it, and to have been
associated with you gentlemen.

Believe me,

Very sincerely yours,

SIDNEY EDWARD MEZES.

I am returning the ten essays by registered mail addressed to Judge Davis.

LETTER OF APPRECIATION

From the California Historical Society

Hon. James D. Phelan,
   Phelan Building,
      San Francisco.

My dear Senator Phelan:

   On behalf of the Publication Committee of the California Historical Society, I wish to thank you for the courtesy of allowing our committee to read the manuscript of Mr. Blake Ross's essay, "The Golden Crucible." We have each of us read this worth-while study with keen interest, and we wish through you to congratulate the author upon his grasp of what may perhaps be termed the "spirit" of California life. We are particularly happy to learn that this important study of the development of California is to be published in book form.

                              Very truly yours,
                                 CARL I. WHEAT,
                    Chairman of Publication Committee.

APPRECIATION

BY ROBERT E. COWAN

*Librarian, William Andrews Clark Library, Los Angeles, California;
First Vice-President, California Historical Society*

I have read with much interest the essay of Mr. Blake Ross, "The Golden Crucible." The title is happily chosen, and as a general abstract of the political, social and economic life of California, this essay (in my opinion) is an excellent and worthy piece of writing. The author possesses a fine command of language and employs his natural fluent and easy diction to the best of purposes; to present the facts correctly and in their logical sequence, and to proffer his deductions and conclusions in a certain literary style most compatible with the tastes and inclinations of the prospective readers thereof.

Historians no doubt will hold it in some degree of disfavor, but they after all are quite unlikely to read it, or perhaps ever to give it countenance. They will continue to extract the n'th root of economics and present their profound cogitations to a harassed public. An oasis is usually the best part of a desert.

"The Golden Crucible" is certainly well written and is comprehensive of much history into which but few readers care to invade deeply.

CRITICISM

BY OSCAR LEWIS

Secretary of the Book Club of California

It is a pleasure to write a few words in appreciation of this essay. Prize contests do not invariably produce the results for which their sponsors hope, and it is a source of satisfaction that in this instance the winning manuscript passes so successfully the tests of interest and of literary quality.

It seems to me that "The Golden Crucible" is an excellent piece of work. It has in abundance a quality that much historical writing lacks; that is, vitality. In order to impart life to a chronicle of bygone events, to make the past live again, two elements, imagination and enthusiasm, are required; and both are here present. One cannot read a page of the essay without discovering how large a part these play in the reality of the narrative—imagination that clothes the bare bones of historical fact with the flesh and blood of reality; enthusiasm which sharpens the impression and adds the touch of life that makes the real interesting. No one who makes such an approach to California history is likely to write dryly, for the dramatic sweep of the action, and the color and variety of its background, carry the reader forward irresistibly once his interest has been engaged.

The author brings other qualities to his task: a quick, incisive style well suited to his narrative, a talent for apt and picturesque phrases, and a selective sense that leads him unerringly to emphasize significant phases of his story and to avoid the temptation to follow attractive but immaterial byways. The result is in every way worth while. History has been made at an accelerated pace in California during the past three-quarters of a century, and Mr. Blake Ross, without loss to his story, has succeeded in compressing seventy-five very full years into an hour's easy reading. As an outline of the history of the State, and as an incentive to further reading, it is hard to see how it could be improved upon.

PREFACE

In writing "The Golden Crucible," it seemed to me that in the Californian cosmos, one might see recapitulated the major trends of the historical process, and I thought it likely that viewed in retrospect, Californian history might be seen as an epitome of all human history.

At the outset my treatment of the subject was conditioned by the idea of history as essentially an impersonal process, with man as the instrument rather than the molder of destiny . . . This idea of impersonality led me to emphasize events rather than names, which was in accord with the suggestion embodied in the announcement of the contest: "Episodes in chronological order are better than biography." I left out the names of the human actors in the scenes, not because 1 thought they were unimportant but because I thought the larger social and economic movements of which they were only parts, were more important. It seemed to me that in a short essay it was more important to state what was done than to describe those who did it.

B. R.

FOREWORD

BY MRS. FREDERICK H. COLBURN

Chairman James D. Phelan Prize Historical Essay Contest

American California has been given too little credit for the splendid standardization of its varied industries; its fine school systems; its libraries, its distinct place in literature and allied arts and its solid building of a great Commonwealth. Very little has been written of the activities from the Seventies to the Nineties. This period was less colorful than the first half of the past century. To partly remedy this defect I induced Senator James D. Phelan to offer two prizes dealing with this less known development.

The following is the official announcement of the Prize Essay Contest:

"An essay that will be an historical sketch of the larger significant phases of California history from 1850 to 1905, and an interpretation of them. The period before 1850 should not be included, except as background, if desired. An essay is a prose poem and should be written in classic English. Episodes in chronological order are better than biography, although names and dates may be included. The essence of the Period of Achievement is what is wanted.

"One thousand dollars will be given for the best essay; five hundred for second prize. Essays must contain from ten thousand to fifteen thousand words. Contest closes November 15, 1928.

"What Californians did with the gold taken from the mines is the greatest achievement ever accomplished by any people possessed of sudden riches. This is one of the most stimulating and inspiring epochs in history. Unearned wealth brings two reactions: Lazy self-indulgence or wild dissipation. The former causes decay, the second destroys moral fiber; California had no such experience. The men and women receiving Nature's bounties accepted the responsibility entailed. They set about founding a Commonwealth based on freedom and justice and having a classical background.

"California was a shut-in community from the coming

of the first Americans until the building of the Central Pacific Railroad in 1869. This was an epoch-making event.

"California came into the Union a free state, breaking a deadlock in opinion. Its gold production strengthened materially the cause of the Union.

"The contest is under the auspices of San Francisco Branch, League of American Pen Women, Mrs. Frederick H. Colburn, president. Contestants are to consider the first paragraph of this announcement as the full direction to guide them.

"Manuscripts must be submitted anonymously. A sealed envelope with the title of the essay on the outside must contain the name and address of the author, with return postage placed in the sealed envelope. The prize-winning essays shall belong to San Francisco Branch, League of American Pen Women. The judges shall consist of well-known men of letters outside of this organization. All manuscripts should be sent to Mrs. Frederick H. Colburn, 757 Sutter Street, San Francisco, California; Apartment 305. Telephone Prospect 5241.

"The judges for the James D. Phelan Prize Essay Contest are Hon. John F. Davis, past-grand president, Native Sons of the Golden West; Mr. Charles S. Cushing, past-president of the Society of California Pioneers; Professor Herbert E. Bolton, Department of History, University of California; Professor Henry Meade Bland, State Teacher's College, San Jose, and Poet Laureate of California; Mr. Boutwell Dunlap, of the California Historical Society and an acknowledged authority on early history of the State.

"Professor Sidney E. Mezes, president of the University of New York City, will pass final judgment on the best ten essays submitted to him by the local committee. Judge John F. Davis will be chairman of the local committee. The judges have been carefully chosen, and each one adds something to the fitness required. The essays winning the prizes must be literature as well as history."

It was the wish of Senator Phelan, that Professor Mezes should be named the final judge. The local judges were my own selection. All of them served faithfully with unflagging enthusiasm. Satisfaction over results must be attributed to their fine judgment, and I wish especially to commend the meticulous care exercised by Judge John F. Davis as local chairman. Professor Mezes, born at Belmont, California, made the selection of the winning essays while at a health resort in Grasse, France, away from all possible outside influence, and with nothing but a number to guide him.

To Arthur H. Chamberlain, editor of the Overland Monthly magazine, thanks and appreciation are due for publishing the winning essay in serial form, in its columns, and for giving the official rules a wide publicity and approval.

Fifteen hundred copies of the official notices were sent through the mails. I answered two hundred and fifty direct inquiries and there were one hundred and twenty-five libraries in the State which posted these notices on their bulletin boards. The organizations of the Native Sons and Native Daughters of the Golden West each sent out two hundred copies of the rules; the Society of California Pioneers and the California Writers Club each mailed two hundred and fifty copies of the official notices to their members while the eight branches of the League of American Pen Women in the State sent every member the printed data.

All of the newspapers from San Diego to Sacramento from the beginning of the contest to the present time, printed almost daily some item of California History of the period involved. This will prove to be of incalculable value to the future historian in need of source material of special localities and events. The newspaper files from 1927 to date will form a very valuable addition to the extensive Californiana already preserved. Each and every one of these publications are entitled to the hearty thanks of all lovers of California history.

It was while listening in on the radio talks of Mr. Joseph Henry Jackson broadcasting book reviews over KGO that Blake Ross heard of the essay contest. Mr. Jackson's efforts stimulated much interest in the essay contest and so did the weekly announcements of the rules over KPO from the San Francisco studio and the equally effective talks on the subject over station KFI, Los Angeles.

To the San Diego Union, the Los Angeles Times, the San Jose Mercury, the San Francisco Chronicle, Examiner, Daily News, Call-Bulletin, the Oakland Tribune, and the Sacramento Bee are acknowledgments due for repeated publicity and hearty co-operation. Many of the Eastern literary magazines gave space to the rules governing the contest.

In the year of time consumed in securing the fifty-eight essays submitted, almost every state in the Union was represented. The number of men and women competing were about evenly divided. It was altogether fine of each of them to devote the time and energy necessary to compete for either of the prizes. I consider all of them co-workers in the attempt to depict the rather neglected phases of our common heritage and am grateful for their assistance.

Mr. Blake Ross, winner of the first prize, was born in Maine in 1900. He came to California in 1912, went to school in San Diego, and enlisted in the Students' Army Training Corps at the University of Redlands. In 1921 he entered the University of California and in 1923 his health failed. From the University he removed to Arroyo Sanitarium, Livermore, California, then later to the U. S. Veterans' Hospital just over the hill, where he wrote "The Golden Crucible." It is hard to realize that this is his first effort, and that he wrote propped up in bed with a writing pad on his knees and no reference library at hand. However, he made good use of the California source material of the State Library, Sacramento, through the library connected with the U. S. Veterans' Hospital, where he lived for four years.

The second essay, "The State Everybody Loves, California," was written by Professor Rockwell D. Hunt, dean of the Graduate School, University of Southern California, who is an authority on history and economics. He is a native Californian, a graduate of Johns Hopkins University. His history, "California, the Golden," is a text book for young students in many of our public schools. His latest venture, "A Short History of California," written in collaboration with Nellie Van de Grift Sanchez, has been highly praised by Senator Phelan in a carefully written criticism published in the New York Saturday Review of Literature.

For the many opportunities afforded me of speaking before Women's Clubs in the Bay region on the plan of the prize essays and for numerous talks over radio on the same subject am I deeply grateful. Hearty co-operation from many sources makes this labor of love a delightful task. It has been a joy to work with Senator Phelan. Through his generosity the copyright of "The Golden Crucible" becomes the property of San Francisco Branch, League of American Pen Women. The proceeds from the sale of this book will be used by the Pen Women to found and help maintain a Fellowship Fund with which to assist their members in distress.

THE GOLDEN CRUCIBLE

"Through all the complex facts that are here set down in their somewhat confused order I have felt running the one thread of the process whereby a new and great community first came to a true consciousness of itself."

—Josiah Royce.

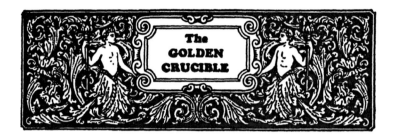

The
GOLDEN
CRUCIBLE

I

THE history of American California has a threefold significance. It has significance for the Californian because it tells him something of his past; for the American because it reveals the process by which a frontier community grew from chaotic beginnings into an American state; for the historian because it epitomizes the history of the race.

The Californian may bask pridefully and with reason in the reflected glory of his predecessors, and perhaps thereby increase a little his own stature, but the historian is not so much concerned with the exploits of provincial heroes. He sees them only as individual manifestations of the whole process of history.

The American takes proper pride in viewing the State's development as a typical example of the American spirit working to transform a frontier of the pioneer into an integral part of the whole nation. The historian and philosopher, with wider vision, sees that California's history is of universal rather than local or national significance. His view comprehends the history as a whole. He sees almost before his eyes a recapitulation of the universal processes of history that have brought us from primitive beginnings to the complex civilization of our own day.

Before him in rapid review pass the successive stages of the social evolution of mankind. Beginning with the free and nomadic life of the individual hunter it progresses through the following stages of racial development: The migration of a people; the invasion of an alien land and the conquest of its inhabitants; the establishment of a pastoral and agricultural way of life momentarily interrupted by the miner and then reëstablished as the basic economy of the State; the setting up of government; the growth of trade and commerce and the consequent reaching out for social and economic contacts with other states; and a temporary rounding out of the process by the introduction of machine technology.

Coincident with this economic growth may be seen a corresponding development of social institutions. Old habits of life are modified to suit the new environment. New problems bring forth new ideas. New social and economic needs bring forth new patterns of behavior. Political concepts change with changed conditions. Law itself proves far less than immutable. Individual activities imposed by the necessities of everyday life grow into social habits, which in turn by the sanction of common usage are elevated at last into the authority of written law.

One sees that the historical process is as complex as life itself. It is the sum total of all the social, economic, and political processes through which we have come out of the past into the present. In the development of American California one sees that process in operation. It can be studied as it manifests itself in the activities of the men who lived and worked in the Californian past. We have a record of their accomplishments and we know something of their failures. If we do not always know the motives for their actions we nevertheless can frequently discern the consequences thereof. The events recorded in their history help us to a better comprehension of the historical development of California as an American state—that complex process through which an uncoördinated group of individuals became in the course of time a community of human lives which by the beginning of the twentieth century had brought California close to the fulfillment of its destiny: social and economic union with the rest of the American Commonwealth.

In the wide retrospective survey afforded us by these records of the past, we see that the forces leading toward this final integration of American California had their origin far back in time. A century before the Pacific Railroad closed the frontier period in California, forces were in motion which were to draw California out of Mexican control and into American. Events of widely different origin, and contemporaneously unrelated, developed consequences and ramifications which prepared the way and set the stage for the American acquisition of California.

The
GOLDEN
CRUCIBLE

II

PONTIAC in the spring of 1769 was dead in St. Louis with a hatchet in his brain. Pontiac was dead, who had been the Indian leader of a futile uprising against white invaders of the Ohio Valley. . . . Fifteen hundred miles to the west, Padre Junipero Serra was toiling up the long peninsula of Baja California. He came at last to the bay of San Diego. Two hundred and twenty-seven years earlier the California Indians had seen Cabrillo set foot on their shores to claim their land for his King. Now Serra had come to claim their souls for his God.

Six years later the shot heard 'round the world roused no echo in California. No alien sound could disturb its quiet. California was a dream at the close of the long Spanish day—a last effort to extend the Spanish frontier in the New World. Especially, California was Serra's dream. A few more hours would see its end: how few, Serra did not know as he labored at Carmel and dreamed within his dream of the new mission to be established the following year on the western shore of the bay of St. Francis.

Less than three months after the declaration of American independence the Spanish flag floated for the first time over the new presidio at San Francisco. That same year, while Serra built in California and redcoat and rebel fought in the East, Captain Cook's two vessels left harbor at Plymouth, England. Reaching Nootka Sound after a prolonged stay among the islands of the South Sea, they found the Alaskan Indians eager to trade with them. A few trivial articles were bartered by the English, for a variety of rich furs. From this unpremeditated beginning sprang up the important Northwest fur trade, which first brought American trading interests to the coast of California.

A few more years went by. Indian neophytes in California bent to their tasks within the walls of eight missions and in 1784 Serra was as dead as Pontiac. . . . Two thousand miles eastward, the people of the United States of America, hardly yet conscious of their new freedom, turned their faces toward the West. They remembered Ohio and the Tennessee country, and already they were following the trails of Clark and Boone. . . . On the other side of the world, at the port of entry for Canton, a Yankee supercargo from Boston sold his vessel's freight and opened for New England commerce the rich Chinese trade that was to send the American flag over the waters of two oceans.

It was not long thereafter that the first American to set foot on Californian soil arrived at Monterey. The mark of death was on him, however, and though his presence foretold the inevitable end of the Spanish dream there were none to read the augury—not even the padres who on September 13, 1791, inscribed on the pages of the mission register the record of his burial. Four years later another American, "a young man of the Boston nation," put in his appearance at Santa Barbara and expressed a desire to become a Christian and a Californian. But he was a foreigner. Despite his praiseworthy ambitions, the local authorities promptly deported him.

The course of history was not to be so lightly turned aside. The very next year, 1796, the first American ship to touch the coast of California

dropped anchor beyond the surf at Monterey.
At the same time, beyond the western horizon,
foreign merchantmen in the Chinese trade were
even then turning their prows toward the waters
of the Pacific Northwest where Russia controlled
the Alaskan coast and its valuable fur trade.

The Californians viewed with some concern
the possible encroachment of the Russians down
the coast, but in the few and distant sails of
Yankee merchantmen and fur traders they saw
no cause for anxiety. On the contrary, not long
after the nineteenth century opened they were
giving occasional if guilty welcome to American
ships whenever they broke the laws of Spain by
bringing foreign goods into the Province of
California. Meanwhile, through the purchase of
Louisiana, the United States of America crossed
the barrier of the Mississippi, doubled its area,
and extended its western boundary a thousand
miles nearer the Pacific.

The Californians were not alarmed, a year or
so later, when the Lewis and Clark expedition
laid down one more thread of American influence in the West. They were not interested in
Captain Shaler's report in 1808 that in settling
California, "the Spaniards have removed every
obstacle out of the way of an invading enemy;

. . . they have done everything . . . to render California an object worthy the attention of the great maritime powers . . ." Nor were they aroused by his opinion that "the conquest of this country would be absolutely nothing; it would fall without an effort to the most inconsiderable force." These events awakened no apprehension in California, since Californians knew nothing at all about them.

Despite the infrequent (and illegal) arrival of some fur trader, merchantman, or whaler, the Province of California in the early years of this century was still a world apart. Serra was dead, but his successors had inherited his dream and were carrying on his work. If the dream were fading a little before the advance of material prosperity, the work nevertheless was going steadily forward. By 1820 thousands of Indian converts were laboring in the workrooms, fields, and orchards of twenty missions. Except for a few Russian colonists far north on the Californian coast, no tangible evidence of foreign aggression had yet appeared. Within the Province, only thirteen foreigners were recorded, and of these, only three were Americans.

So when the year 1822 brought Mexican independence, most Californians felt that the loss of the Spanish flag was more than compensated for by the removal of the trade restrictions that had prevented the economic development of the Province. In this year they welcomed the establishment of branch offices in Monterey of an English and an American firm, both of which had been attracted by the commercial possibilities of the hides and tallow produced from the mission herds.

While the "Boston ships" were carrying California's leather to the shoe manufacturers of Massachusetts and Connecticut, and her name to all the East, the Californians were still turning their gaze suspiciously toward the north, where the Russians in 1812 had established a fort and trading post on Bodega Bay. The Californians could not see over the ramparts of the Sierra toward the East, where the American tide already had overflowed the western shores of the Mississippi. They could not see the small band of colonists that were following Stephen Austin and the frontiersmen into Texas. Even if they could have seen, they would have watched with complacent unconcern over the thousand miles of mountains and desert that lay between. . . . Above all, they could not see the American trappers who were hunting the beaver along all the rivers of the north and west.

These trappers, outriders of the pioneer advance, forerunners of the frontier, slipped silently along Indian trails and up the banks of lonely rivers where the old quiet was disturbed for the first time by the crack of their long rifles. They followed Lewis and Clark and explored further the Northwest and the Oregon country. They penetrated the Southwest and prepared the way for caravans over the trail from Missouri to Santa Fe. They followed western streams to their headwaters in the Rocky Mountains and went over them, always toward the West. Once beyond the Rockies, they found themselves in an unknown desolation, the Great Basin, a waste of desert, rock, and gray sagebrush, criss-crossed by many mountains and few rivers.

One of these rivers flowed south and west. In 1826 a small band of American trappers made their way down this river to its junction with a still grander stream. They followed the Colorado southwestward until they left its rocky banks and struck off across the desert, going toward the West. Through sand and scattered clumps of sagebrush and cacti they picked their way until they came once more to mountains. They found a pass and broached the last barrier between them and the brown and gold valley that lay outspread below them. Through the November haze that laid purple shadows in the distant canyons and mingled with the golden glow of grain fields they saw the softened outlines of a little group of mission buildings lying in the valley before them. They approached the buildings and were greeted by grey-gowned Padre Sanchez, of the San Gabriel mission. He gave them a generous welcome, not quite realizing that in the person of Jedediah Smith, their leader, the "Manifest Destiny" of the United States had crossed California's last defense.

On all sides the net of American influence was closing in on California. Off her coast, Yankee ships left foaming wakes that shone white for a moment and were gone—but in the wet, dark shadows of their hulls they laid down lines of subtle force which were eventually to draw California into the American Union. The shadow of their flags fell on water and the waves were restless. A few more years and that shadow found the certain land.

While events marched thus inexorably upon California, internal forces of dissolution were at work to reinforce the social and economic advance of American interest and American purpose. Secularization of the missions came in 1834. Civil authorities assumed control of all the mission holdings. The lands were sold or leased; the mission herds were sold, stolen, or killed; and the Indian neophytes forsook the solace of Christianity for the peace of their native hills. Serra's dream was ended. The Californian world was near to breaking up, to be held together for only a few more years by Governor Alvarado's strong hand.

But Alvarado was striving against fate. The very year he assumed control in California, Sam Houston at San Jacinto broke Mexico's failing hold on Texas. In so doing he but accelerated the already swift march of events toward California, lying between Sierra and the sea, last refuge of an old world dying.

This was in 1836. By this time a small number of Americans were living in California. Some of them were hunters turned pioneer in the sparsely settled valleys. A few were wandering up and down the country, turning their hands to the needs of the moment. Others were come to try their fortunes in such commerce as the Province supported—"but whether the foreigners blew in from the sea or drifted across the sand, those who remained became to all intents and purposes, as the 'hijos del pais' "— sons of the country. They were assimilated by the Californians and lived their life.

It was soon over. California even in those days was a potent name throughout the East. All maritime and commercial New England knew it. Readers throughout the nation saw it in "Two Years Before the Mast." Newspapers carried it linked with the name of Oregon. It had been sounded within the Capitol at Washington. There was a certain magic in its syllables,—and pioneers on the western prairies were restless.

In May, 1841, sixty-nine emigrants left the Missouri frontier, knowing that they were going to California, and knowing only that California lay west. On the fourth of the following November, John Bidwell arrived with his little party at an American ranch near the foot of Mount Diablo. At last and inevitably the American frontier had reached California.

The American flag followed with synchronous precision, and came, logically enough, from the sea, where that flag had been seen so often before from the Californian coast. Before

Bidwell had spent his first year in the Province, an American commodore in Peru, misled by ambiguous dispatches and under the mistaken impression that Mexico and his country were at war, set sail with all speed for California. He feared that his British rivals in the Pacific might reach and occupy the Province before he could do so himself. Entering Monterey harbor and seeing no sign of British warships he promptly demanded the surrender of Monterey, a demand that was as promptly complied with. The Commodore ran up the American flag over the bewildered city. The next day he pulled it down again.

Yet Commodore Jones made no essential mistake. His actions were merely a bit premature. In California, American immigrants continued to defy the law by illegally entering foreign territory. In Texas, the Republic throve mightily, and was annexed to the United States in 1845. The following year, while an ambitious band of American patriots "captured" the hamlet of Sonoma north of the bay of San Francisco, the United States and Mexico fought to defend their national honors. Then over Monterey the Stars and Stripes fluttered proudly— and now permanently.

California was ceded to the United States when the Treaty of Guadalupe Hidalgo brought formal peace on the second of February, 1848. Nine days before this, Sutter's hired man made his famous discovery, and American immigration, that had been trickling into California for seven years, became almost over night a flood. In its torrential course it agitated the nation from one end to the other, and drew into its main current tributary streams from every state in the Union. The rest of the world was almost as profoundly affected by the golden spell. California, long a name only, had become again a symbol.

Its glittering promise raised the hope of every man who wanted another chance at Fortune's wheel. And who did not? A hundred thousand set out for California in '49. Most of them got there—around the Horn, through the pestilential swamps of the Isthmus, across the deserts of New Mexico and the Colorado, over the Rockies and down the arid slopes of the Great Basin. But the majority of the American Argonauts came overland. It was a march. Slow hooves of oxen cut the prairie turf. Great wheels turned endlessly toward the West. Fifty thousand

Americans marching beside their oxen and their wagons carried their aureate hopes along the muddy Platte, up the prairie highlands to the Rockies, over them and down into the dry desolation of the Great Basin. They passed Salt Lake and with the weariness of months upon their shoulders, worked their various ways across the rock and sand. Deprivation walked with them. Starvation, thirst, and exhaustion followed. Death Valley got its name.

Yet most endured. Such is the power of a symbol. In a few short months it accomplished what Imperial Spain had been unable to do in three centuries. It populated California. It brought into the land a hundred thousand young and eager men, obsessed with the lust for gain and perhaps a little mad, but quite able to move mountains and build a State.

In the Autumn of 1850 California was admitted into the American Union as a free state. The long march of years was nearly over. Hundreds of thousands of white men had trampled Pontiac's unconsidered grave, always marching toward the West. They moved in unsuspecting unison with the processes of fate. When President Fillmore traced his signature to the bill of admission, he merely gave official sanction to an inevitable consequence of a process begun indefinitely in the past and continuing indefinitely into the future.

III

CALIFORNIA in 1850 was a state merely by virtue of an act of Congress. It was far from being a state in the widest sense of the term. It was unformed as a whole. There was little social or economic coherence among its various elements. Its population was a heterogeneous mixture of all types and nationalities. Although it had geographical form and political reality, socially and economically California was an abstraction—a whirling confusion of conflicting forces centering on a promise of things yet to be rather than on things already existent. Before California could attain final structure as a state, the economic, social, and political elements of its whole life needed to be resolved from the confusion of 1850 into the balanced order of a half-century later.

Such a transformation was soon effected. It was an amazing phenomenon. As the march of events that brought California into the Union revealed the historical process in its more obvious aspects, so the internal development of California during the first half-century of State-hood disclosed the workings of that process in subtle detail. One sees social order and economic stability growing out of primary confusion. The process is complex, and its intricacies and rami-fications are without end; yet its main phases may be described and analyzed by dividing the factors of this gradual evolution into two gen-eral categories: those furthering the growth of order and unity, and those resisting or opposing it. Therefore in studying the progress of Cali-fornia during this period, events must be evalu-ated according to their effectiveness in advanc-ing or retarding the final integration of the State. Local events, however interesting in themselves, must be disregarded except as they affect the development of the State as a whole.

In 1850, however, California was by no means a whole. It was unorganized and inco-herent. It is true that it had a certain political unity, and an organic law provided by the State constitution of 1849. The machinery of govern-ment was already set up, though it would be

some time before it would function smoothly—
or honestly. In addition to this kind of political
unity, the State possessed physical form. It was
a geographical whole, carved out of the Mexican cession of 1848. Its boundaries were fixed,
enclosing a million acres of valley, desert, and
mountain, with a coast line that curved a thousand miles from the Oregon line to the Silver
Strand at Coronado. Yet these two things, the
one physical and the other political, provided
the merest outline for the complex pattern of
communal life that was to develop so quickly.
Within this bare outline, all the elements of the
future commonwealth were unorganized, obscure, inchoate.

Consider the social geography. In the first
year of Statehood virtually all the population of
California was divided into three separate sections. From San Jose and southward down the
coast from Monterey to San Diego, some ten
thousand native Californians and naturalized
foreigners lived in the settlements of the old
regime. San Francisco, at the northernmost
point of this coastal division, was in effect an
independent principality, holding economic
sway by the Golden Gate. There, twenty or

thirty thousand restless atoms of human energy whirled about in clouds of sand, fog and frenzied activity.

One hundred miles east of San Francisco lay the third center of population, the gold mining districts in the ravines and gulches seaming the western slopes of the Sierra. With the exception of the Trinity River region in the north, inhabited by some two thousand gold seekers, the important mining activity of the State was carried on in a territory about fifty miles in width by two hundred miles in length, from Mariposa County northward to the Feather River. Here, in an area of less than seven per cent of the total area of the State, two-thirds of all the people in California were grubbing in the earth.

Besides this geographical division, there was a corresponding lack of unity in the social structure. Three main classes of the population might have been discerned. First, but few in number and utterly unimportant from the Americans' point of view, were the ten or twelve thousand native Californians. These were the descendants of the original Spanish and Mexican stock. With them, and living their life in town or rancho, were a few foreigners who had become naturalized citizens of California before 1846. In the second class, and perhaps even less in number, were the Americans of pioneer stock who had come into California during the decade preceding the gold rush. They had come for the sole purpose of taking up new land and had settled mostly in the valleys north of San Francisco Bay, or inland within the Sacramento Valley. They had temporarily deserted their holdings after the discovery of gold, when most of them joined the rush to the mines. Finally, and greatly outnumbering all these others, was the heterogeneous mob that had come primarily as a consequence of the gold discovery. Over one hundred thousand came in 1849 and the first part of 1850. Of these, over half were native Americans, the majority of them being from the mid-western frontiers. It is well known, also, that the older communities of the East were well represented by men from all the walks of life. In addition to these Americans, there was an amazing number of foreigners among the gold-seekers. Ten years later, one might have seen two foreign-born men for every three Americans, and there seems to be no reason for doubting that the ratio was nearly as high during the first years of the decade. This great proportion of foreigners was an important factor in determining the social consciousness of the new State.

Because so much has been said about the great numbers coming to the State in the rush of '49 the impression prevails that within a few years California became densely populated. Nothing could be farther from the truth. In the year following 1849, all the miners in the State could have been seated in the Stanford Stadium or the Los Angeles Coliseum of today. The entire population of San Francisco and the Bay district could have stood on the playing field, and around its borders there would have been ample room for the few thousand old inhabitants scattered in the four hundred miles of territory along the southern coast. No human being except the Indian aborigine would have been left elsewhere in the state's 156,000 square miles.

The economic life of California rode high— if somewhat precariously—on the flood of gold from the mines. Most of this golden stream found its way down the Sierran ravines to the Sacramento and San Joaquin rivers, and down them to San Francisco. There it was exchanged for supplies to be taken back over the same route to the mines—except when the miners themselves brought their dust to town. In the latter event, their returns were less tangible, though the economics of gambling, wine and women operate just as effectively as the more ordinary forms of exchange.

Besides this swelling current of liquid wealth the city was enriched by another economic stream. As noted by Cleland, "every shipload and overland party of immigrants brought a new demand for food, lodging, drink and mining equipment to the San Francisco merchants."

San Francisco was the nerve center and economic heart of the new life. Sensitive to the golden impulse from the mines, it translated this stimulus into commercial action, and imported all sorts of goods, which were then sent out to the mining towns. The new city of Sacramento was perhaps the most important inland distributing point for this trade, though the merchants of Stockton on the San Joaquin river obtained their share of the trade that filtered in both directions through their city. From these secondary centers of trade the supplies went north, south, and east to the mining towns, which supplied the local wants of the "diggings."

Old California, somnolent along the southern

coast, felt the stimulus of this new energy and made feeble efforts to respond. Nevertheless it profited but indirectly and relatively little from the State's new wealth. A few immigrants increased the trade of local merchants to a certain extent, but this scanty growth of population was not comparable to the vast influx into central California, just as the meager profits of the South's only important industry—cattle raising —was not to be spoken of wherever the magic sound of "gold" could be heard. A full generation would pass before southern California would begin to come into its own.

It will be seen that there was a want of economic coördination in the State. San Francisco, the southern California cities, and those of the central valley and the mines provided nuclei of economic activity throughout the State. Yet economic coördination was delayed for many years, for several reasons. First, and important, was the lack of proper methods of communication. No roads connected the southern and central part of the State, and if it had not been for the avenues of traffic provided naturally by the two great rivers flowing into San Francisco Bay, the northern section would also have been without adequate lines of communication. At this time, saddle or pack horses were the only means of land transportation. On the rivers, craft of all descriptions were pressed into service to carry passengers and goods from San Francisco to the interior, while outside the surf line along the ocean shore two or three small steamboats paddled up and down the coast between San Francisco and the undeveloped ports of the south. Several years were to elapse before the pressure of social and economic necessity brought roads and stagelines, the telegraph, and last of all the railroad.

Another reason for the delay in economic development was still more important, and fundamental. It was, simply, that California had to import every single item of the most common needs of life. California had nothing but gold. Yet gold cannot be eaten or worn, and it cannot shelter. Flour had to be imported from Chile, sugar and potatoes from the Hawaiian Islands, rice and tea from China. Even lumber at first was imported. California produced nothing. It did not even produce gold. It found it. There was nothing economically creative in the State in 1850.

Several factors besides the two already noted were responsible for this lack of creative effort.

There was, for example, the factor of time. It is obvious that even under the most favorable circumstances little more could have been accomplished than was actually done in the first years following the gold rush. Then there was the almost universal obsession with the idea of gold. Gold offered immediate and tangible gain. Gold was the object of all desire. Gold was God. Why gain it indirectly through other pursuits when one might dig it for himself, or at the furthest, take it directly from the miner? When one adds the fact that the vast majority of the newcomers came to California with the express intention only of getting gold to take back with them to their respective homes in the East, and not with the idea of making new homes in California, it is not surprising that at first so little was done to develop the other natural resources of the State.*

Nevertheless, despite the prevalence of this attitude, there was a surprisingly large number of American immigrants who preferred land to gold. Many of them took to the mines solely with the idea of digging enough gold to buy or develop land, either within the State, or

_____
*Of course the lack of labor and the smallness of the population as a whole was fundamental to the general problem of State development.

"back East," where the family homestead lay under the shadow of first, second, or third mortgages. A troublesome number, however, had already settled on land in California. The problems and confusion arising from the activities of these squatters were serious obstacles to the development of the whole State.

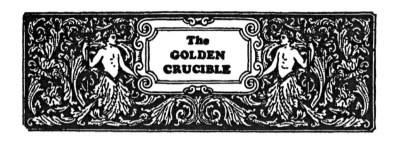

The
GOLDEN
CRUCIBLE

IV

THE AMERICAN settlers wanted land. Much of the land they wanted, and actually "squatted" on, was owned or claimed under original grants of the Mexican government. Out of this situation grew the conflict between the settler and the grantee. "The land question in California," says Joseph Ellison, "was of a three-fold character: the adjudication upon the validity of land titles claimed under the Mexican government; the disposition of the public domain; the control and disposition of the gold fields." The second and third of these problems were worked out in the course of time, but the first was an immediate problem, and a serious one. Stated briefly, the trouble had its origin in the conflicting Mexican and American attitudes toward land, with respect to its value and use. In Mexican days land was virtually worthless. It was used only for grazing the herds of cattle that provided the sole California industry. Since there were relatively few inhabitants there was no need to restrict the size or the number of the grants. After the missions were secularized in 1834 almost any reputable citizen could obtain land by grant from the government. As a consequence, when the Province passed into American control in 1846, much, but by no means all, of the desirable land in the coast districts was claimed under titles granted by the Spanish and Mexican governments.

The Americans, on the other hand, held a quite different conception of the land. So, to quote Ellison again, it is not surprising that trouble arose, "with the influx of land-hungry settlers from the western states. They had been accustomed to small holdings with fixed boundaries, and to them squatting upon uncultivated land was a perfectly respectable American practice in settling a new territory. These Americans came to California with the belief that, except for a few settlements confined to the coast, all the land in the territory was public domain, and that, as in the other territories which had been opened to settlement, they might preempt a tract of land by squatter's rights. Hence great was their disappointment when they found thousands of acres of the best lands lying uncultivated and claimed by a small number of landowners under some inchoate loose grant of the benighted Mexican government."

During the Mexican regime, one person could be granted a very large tract, often one as large as eleven leagues. By any standard this was a princely acreage, amounting to more than seventy-five square miles. One of the most famous was the Peralta grant, which covered the sites of Berkeley, Oakland, and Alameda. Sutter's domain along the Sacramento was also a most valuable and important grant. Other grants covered areas in the valleys north and south of San Francisco Bay and in the valleys and along the shore from Santa Cruz to San Diego.

According to the law of nations and confirmed by the Treaty of Guadalupe Hidalgo, the title to all property thus legally acquired was to remain valid under American rule. There is no question as to the integrity of this principle. In practice, however, it was found difficult to apply it in all cases. The boundaries of many grants had been vaguely defined, and it often was impossible to describe a grant for the purpose of proving validity of title. The Californians them-selves in many instances did not know the precise extent of their property. "Consequently," as Ellison notes, "there was a large number of land claims varying from one to eleven leagues square, that were indefinite with respect to boundaries." Vague boundaries and other irregularities thus threatened in many instances to unsettle titles. Fraudulent claims and forged grants soon made their appearance, to increase the general confusion and bitterness.

The reality and the seriousness of the land problem cannot be doubted. One of the first pieces of national legislation affecting California, the Land Act of 1851, grew out of it. As the Act affected California it provided for a board of three commissioners to pass upon the validity of all claims to land granted by the Spanish or Mexican government. For the present, the effect of the land problem and the Act of 1851 on the course of State life can be anticipated in the following words of Eldredge: "By questioning the title the law made the land hard to sell and the owner in order to raise money for taxes, support, and defense (of title) was obliged to part with a good portion at a fraction of its value . . . thus vast tracts fell into the hands of lawyers and speculating land sharpers." The result was a concentration in a few hands of "a great part of the agricultural lands," and this of course "worked great detriment to the development of the state."

V

IT was inevitable that grave problems of
social and moral order should grow out of
all these uncertainties in early Californian
life. The social order of the State was quite unorganized. In the heterogeneous mass of fortune
hunters there was scarcely one with any sense
of social responsibility. Individualism, reckless
and selfish, dominated the social scene. Each
one was seeking his own fortune. He had neither
time nor inclination to worry over his neigh-
bor's troubles. He had no concern for posterity,
his own or any other's. The present, golden and
immediate, was all he thought of and all he
desired. There was, it is true, a certain unani-
mity of action among the mass that might
mislead a casual observer into the belief that
from the first men worked together. But there
was no true social order among them. They were
actuated by the same motive that leads flies to

cluster upon a trickle of molasses. They had the singleness of purpose characteristic of those insects, and no more social coherence. They lacked, in Josiah Royce's telling phrase, "a sense of mutual destinies."

Only the early settlers and a few business men (and of course the native Californians, who for the moment did not count) had any genuine interest in the future of the State. And they for the moment were submerged in the tumultuous life centering upon the idea of gold and individual fortune. So it is not strange that violence and crime made their appearance as social manifestations of the universal want of order in the new State. Yet there is this to be noted: the violence was in general sporadic, a manifestation of individual caprice. It was a misdirection of free energy, not the explosive violence that results from social restriction.

Crime was primitive and elemental. Theft and murder were by far the most common crimes, as they are the most primitive, and the most simple. Both violence and crime, like the society that fostered them, were individualistic. It is notable, too, that as crime became organized such organization occurred where society already possessed at least embryonic form—as in San Francisco, where political knavery flourished, or in Southern and Central California, where organized bands of highwaymen and horse and cattle thieves soon enough made their appearance.

Even the punishment occasionally meted out by "society" was essentially individualistic in its nature. Miners' meetings that measured popular justice by the rope's length were not judicial manifestations of an established order. They were merely temporary coalitions of individual units of social energy: not permanent coördinations developed from and resting upon the common interest. It was in San Francisco, the most complex social unit of the State, and therefore with a higher relative need of social coördination, that popular justice as expressed by the Vigilance Committees of 1851 and 1856 reached a relatively more definite coherence, orderliness, and stability of social form.

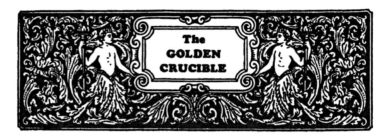

The
GOLDEN
CRUCIBLE

VI

IN ADDITION to the social and economic factors already mentioned, California's isolation from the rest of the nation was of great importance in its effect upon the course of State history. Communication with the East required weeks, and transportation of goods required months. Mail was a month en route from New York via the Isthmus. Merchandise was sent in sailing ships around the Horn, and a six months' voyage was not considered slow. It took four or five months for an emigrant train to cross the mountains and plains west of the Mississippi; and several more if the point of departure was on the Atlantic seaboard.

The two highest mountain ranges in the United States and hundreds of miles of desert and rocky wasteland lay between California and the eastern part of the nation. Consequently the State's relation to the rest of the Union was anomalous. Politically, California was a full-fledged state in the American Union, but economically and socially it was more like a colony characterized by frontier conditions. Hittell states this concisely: "Other new states were in substance merely the expansion of the outer boundaries of older states; but California was essentially a colony and developed as a distinct and for the time being a disconnected organization."

The foregoing brief description of conditions in the California of 1850 indicates the situation and suggests the problem. Here was a vast new state on the western edge of the continent, carved out of the Mexican cession of 1848. Thinly populated, much of it hardly yet explored by its new owners, with the remnant of an alien people and an alien culture in one section, an inchoate metropolis in another, a tumultuous mass of fortune hunters in a third, how was this California to be transformed into the California of the twentieth century—a unified American state and an integral part of the nation?

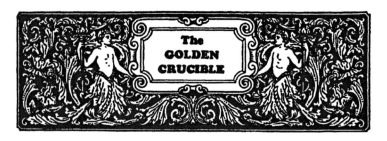

The GOLDEN CRUCIBLE

VII

THINGS are relative to the standards by which they are judged. To say that California in 1850 was unorganized and individualistic is a relative truth. Complete lack of organization is chaos. Absolute individualism is anarchy. There was neither chaos or anarchy in those early days, but there was the great confusion that results from constant and rapid change. California was a society in process of healthy growth and development, not one in process of decay and dissolution. It was a society in which all the rudimentary social and economic elements of State life were in process of development, extension and coördination.

Of all the conservative forces at work in this process, it is probable that the tendency toward political organization was the most important and the most potent. The American immigrants in California had brought with them a most valuable portion of their social heritage: the political customs and ideals of their American ancestry. The accumulated political experience of the past was theirs to draw upon.

They made quick use of their knowledge. The first State constitution of 1849 is an example of their political proficiency. They showed equal skill in electing and organizing a legislature, and in setting up the machinery for State government. In the cities, also, political organizations were soon effected. Even in the mining camps, as has been suggested, there were loose popular organizations for the punishment of offenses against life or property, and for regulating local mining practices.

But form does not always provide substance. California was, it is true, politically precocious —yet precocity is not maturity, nor is knowledge always synonymous with wisdom. Governmental machinery in a democracy may be set up by the people, but it requires also to be run by the people. This corollary was overlooked by the public in the early days of the State. As a consequence, with the lapse of popular interest in government (through absorption with individual pursuits of fortune) such government as remained effective became inefficient, extravagant, and corrupt. More often than not, courts and judges proved themselves dishonest or incompetent. Police officials became lax in enforcing the law. Not infrequently they were known or suspected to be in connivance with criminals.

Out of such conditions grew the early vigilance committees, organized in various parts of the State. The best known are the committees of 1851 and 1856 in San Francisco. The corrupt and inefficient practices of officials charged with preserving law and order aroused public indignation to such an extent in 1851 that the people became convinced of the need of organizing in self-protection against the forces of disorder. A popular organization was soon formed with a constitution which, as summarized by Hittell, declared that it was their purpose "to sustain the laws when faithfully and properly administered; but they were determined in any and all events that no thief, burglar, incendiary or assassin should any longer escape punishment either by the quibbles of the law, the insecurity of the prisons, the carelessness or corruption of the police or the laxity of those who pretended to administer justice . . . they agreed that the name and style of the association should be the 'Committee of Vigilance' and its object the protection of the lives and property of the citizens and resident of the city of San Francisco."

The Committee soon had opportunity to function. An Australian criminal stole a small iron safe. He was pursued, captured, brought before the Committee, given a fair and orderly trial, convicted, sentenced to death, and hanged —all within five hours. In the course of their activity, the Committee of '51 found it necessary to hang three more criminals, and to warn or banish several score of undesirables. All authorities agree that the actions of this Committee, and of its successor five years later, were characterized by the spirit of fair play and an honest desire for the furtherance of law and order. Their methods, though extra-legal, were effective, and appear to have been justified by the unusual circumstances.

Throughout the State in the early fifties were other committees of vigilance that ranged in nature all the way from lawless mobs that gathered on the impulse of the moment, to social organizations that approached but never equaled the high character of the San Francisco committees. The value and the justification of their acts must remain open to doubt. Nevertheless, drastic measures were often necessary, and since violence seldom begets wisdom, perhaps one should not be too hasty in passing moral judgment on men who resorted to lynch law at a time when governmental authority was a name more often than it was a reality.

In addition to criminals there was another essentially lawless group. These were the squatters, immigrants who took illegal possession of land owned by others. The usual sufferers from this practice were the owners of land under Spanish or Mexican grants. Though many ranchers in outlying districts were annoyed or actually robbed by squatters, it was in the cities that they were the most troublesome. Perhaps the most serious outbreak of squatter violence occurred in Sacramento. That city grew up on a portion of the land granted to Sutter in 1841. According to Hittell, "in the autumn of 1849 there were several thousand immigrants settled on the vacant lots of the town, which had been sold by Sutter and his grantees to other persons; and, asserting that Spanish and Mexican grants were frauds and that no one man had a right to monopolize so much land as Sutter claimed, they declared their intention to retain their lots and resist any and all attempts to dispossess them." The legal owners of the land naturally expressed their opposition. The ensuing conflict in the course of a year or so resulted in riot, bloodshed, and death for a number of those involved.

Other cities and towns had their share of the trouble. Even in southern California, says Cleland, "Conflicts between squatters and ranchers were not at all uncommon, and on more than one occasion whole communities of the new settlers banded themselves together to resist dispossession." It was years before the decisions of the land commission and negotiations between the real owners and the squatters determined the final legal status of all the property under dispute. Meanwhile the agricultural and hence the whole economic development of the State was retarded.

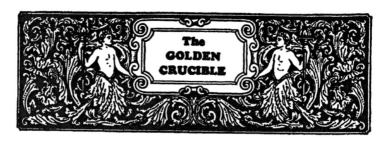

The
GOLDEN
CRUCIBLE

VIII

DURING these early years of uncertainty and excitement the gold mining district was developing a life of its own. It was a life unique with California, and one that deserves the attention of every student of the social process. Out of it grew a culture that in the course of a single generation passed from a first primitive stage of uncoördinated individual activity into one characterized by a highly organized and complex industry. In the few years of its growth it developed social, political, and economic ramifications that directly or indirectly affected almost every phase of the State's growth.

Nearly all the Forty-niners were quite ignorant of mining methods. The social heritage of their past provided them with no common fund of experience to draw upon. They possessed only the most rudimentary conception of mining. Partly by common sense, partly by a little knowledge of pan mining imparted by veteran Mexican miners, and partly by mankind's universal method of progress, trial and error, they gradually developed technical efficiency and social coherence.

At first, the individual miners found it quite practicable to wash out the gold by means of small pans shaken in such a manner as to cause the particles of gold to settle to the bottom. This was the most primitive form of placer mining. Then the small pan of the individual miner gave way to the cradle, or rocker. Soon it proved to be easier and more profitable for two or three men to work together. Labor was divided, and tasks became specialized—one man shoveled pay dirt into the hopper, another poured water into it, and a third rocked the cradle from side to side so that the gold might settle to the bottom and be taken out in the form of "dust." Before long it was discovered that water could be made to do more of the work. Sluice boxes were built and water was diverted into them. The force of the current carried the dirt over the bed of the box, where the gold was caught by cleats nailed across the bottom. This, in many instances, required still greater organization of labor.

A further extension of mechanical equipment came close upon the invention of the sluice box. In 1852, an ingenious miner made use of a small canvas hose to carry water under pressure which when discharged through a tin nozzle and directed against a gold bearing gravel bank, washed the gravel into a sluice box where the gold was recovered. Thus early was hydraulic mining developed in California. From the miner's point of view it was a most successful innovation, and wherever conditions were favorable it was practiced for the next three decades. It was finally prohibited by law, after thousands of acres of fine agricultural land had been ruined by gravel and silt washed down upon it from the mining sites.

With the gradual exhaustion of the placers, quartz mining developed in importance. As time went on it became a highly organized industry requiring the skilled services of geologist, engineer, and metallurgist. To carry on the work stock companies were formed, which by their financial operations affected the lives and happiness of thousands who would never see the mines in which they held shares.

Dependent and correlated industries developed as mining methods became more complicated. First, of course, the miners themselves had to be supplied with the necessities and some of the luxuries of life. Mining equipment had to be designed, manufactured, and brought in. Roads had to be built for the freight and stage lines organized to keep up this traffic between mines and sources of supply. There was need of lumber, so the forests of the State were invaded by logger and millhand. Above all, there was need of water, which in many instances had to be brought to the mines from a distance. Thus it came about that independent organizations were formed to distribute water to mines not supplied by local streams. Great wooden flumes were built, and contracts taken to furnish mining sites with water for a profitable percentage of the gold mined. Water rights became valuable, and, therefore, sources of trouble. So water, since it was an indispensable adjunct to mining, became almost as important as gold, especially in its effect on legislation and the later development of irrigation and hydro-electric power.

Along with the general growth of the mining industry came a corresponding development of laws pertaining to both mineral and water rights. Until 1866 when Congress passed the

Mineral Land Act there was no way of acquiring legal title to a claim or lode, since the Federal Government, which owned the land, had no law governing its disposition. The miner did not own the land outright; he owned merely the right to mine it. Prior occupation and use were the terms on which he held his claim. The rights consequent upon discovery, appropriation, and use were assumed to be fundamental. They were the only rights recognized by the community at large. To protect them, and to establish equitable principles of action that would insure absolute equality of opportunity to all alike, a body of local legislation grew up from the rules and customs of the miners themselves. These local laws were finally incorporated in the common law on the subject.

The doctrine of appropriation and use was soon extended to apply with equal force to the question of water rights. As a result, serious conflicts eventually developed between those who claimed water rights under this new Western doctrine, and those who claimed them under the old English common law doctrine of riparian ownership. Even yet the legal tangle resulting from this conflict has not been entirely straightened out. Irrigation projects, large and small, have been delayed or frustrated because of it, and plans for the development of hydroelectric power have at times been complicated by the same problem.

But whether it concerned gold, or water, the growth of legislation on either subject exemplifies the social process whereby common law doctrines develop. In the words of Crittenden Thornton, on the subject of mining law, "the whole system whether adopted by legislative act or not furnishes a complete example of the growth of the common law upon the subject. First, the customs of the people in regard to the subject; second, the expansion of those customs in regard to lode claims; third, the legislative adoption and the digesting of customs and usages into a compact code of statutes; fourth and last, legislation by the United States providing for a grant of titles in fee to the mines by the government of the United States."

He concludes by remarking that "it is not often that the customs and usages of a people in regard to a certain kind of property have had their origin, development, successful operation, and final adoption by the legislature, both State and Federal, within the lifetime of a single individual," as happened in California.

The
GOLDEN
CRUCIBLE

IX

WHILE the miners were thus organizing their life, and before squatter and grantee had settled their quarrels over the land, the economics of State life was changing even more rapidly than other factors of the general environment. The bright glitter of gold still dazzled most eyes, but underneath the shining surface of events the old economic law of supply and demand was operating as inexorably as ever. The yield of placer gold fell off in the early fifties, and with it, the buying power of the community at large. Imports of goods from the East glutted the local markets. San Francisco merchants found themselves with unsalable stocks. A number of commercial failures occurred, and before the city could adjust itself to the new economic situation, the panic of 1855 had resulted in the disastrous collapse of many of the most important banking houses in the city. The whole State suffered from the depression.

At the same time, however, there were hopeful signs of economic progress. Infant industries appeared, and men who had before worked only as miners or clerks now joined the thin but growing ranks of industrial labor. Agriculture began to develop. Crops became locally diversified. The brown land, scorned at first as arid and barren by newcomers used to the lush green valleys of the East, showed unsuspected fertility. Wheat, planted at a venture, became a certain source of agricultural wealth, and in 1855, when a portion of the crop was exported, was already threatening the economic dominance of gold. In all these shifting economic currents two things stand out: that even then the State was beginning to develop the diversification of interests so necessary for a well balanced economic order; and that the rule of gold in California was nearly over.

California's golden day was indeed a brief one. Within five years of the discovery at Coloma the annual gold yield began to diminish. From an estimated value of over eighty million dollars in 1852, the yield steadily diminished during the next decade. By 1860 the golden current was mingling with other streams of equal economic value. In that year, according to statistics of the California Board of Agriculture, the total value of manufactures exceeded the total gold yield by twenty million dollars. In the following decade a single farm crop, wheat, developed to such an extent that for the rest of the century its annual average value excelled that of all the gold mined in the whole State during the same period.

California's gold, despite its yield of approximately half a billion dollars in the first decade, and another billion in the following half century, never had quite the lasting importance attributed to it by popular fancy. In the early fifties it represented new and easily accessible wealth, and as such it was of almost inestimable importance. Because it was itself the basis of monetary exchange it could be diverted immediately to other purposes without the necessity of intermediate forms of barter. This is doubtless one reason why the State was able to forge ahead so rapidly from the very first. Nevertheless, the coincident development of more varied economic interests marked the early end of gold as the predominant economic factor in the State's progress.

These various economic forces and the social changes they produced are of much greater relative importance than the political activity of men whose thoughts and actions were largely determined by them. The fierce political feuds of the first decade are not especially important in the light of today. Perhaps from our perspective the most important question in early politics was one deemed relatively unimportant at the time it arose—the movement for division of the new State into two parts, one northern, the other southern.

This was a political problem that grew out of an economic situation. Southern California, as has already been noted, gained little profit from the mines. The relatively few land owners in the southern part of the State, whose profits were meager, had to pay the largest share of the State taxes, which were laid on real property. The miners, on the other hand, made great profits from land on which they paid virtually no taxes at all. To make matters worse, the mining counties had almost four times as many representatives in the State legislature as did the six southern counties, which paid twice as much in taxes. As a consequence of this unfair taxation and unequal representation, and because of their belief that the mining and commercial interests of the north had an unbreakable hold on the economic life of the State, the landed interests of the south started the movement for division. They wanted a territorial form of government, as it was less expensive.

From 1851 until the close of the decade, representatives of the southern counties urged this division. In 1859, says Cleland, the State legislature actually "gave its consent to the formation of a separate government for the five counties of San Luis Obispo, Santa Barbara, Los Angeles, San Diego, San Bernardino," and one other county, proposed but not created. That such division of the State did not occur was the result of chance rather than design. The outbreak of the Civil War prevented the Federal legislation necessary to confirm the decision of the legislature. Thus a great sectional conflict that threatened to split the nation was directly responsible for preserving the geographical and political integrity of California, threatened with disruption by divergent sectional interests within the State.

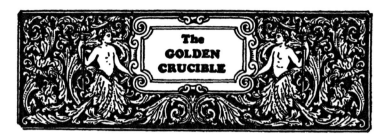

X

WHEN the Civil War began California was still an isolated frontier community, with strong local interests but on the whole indifferent to questions of national policy. As soon as the danger of disunion became apparent, however, Union sentiment prevailed, and despite some Southern sympathy in a few scattered districts, the State never wavered in its allegiance to the Northern cause. Nevertheless, it cannot be said that the fortunes of a war two thousand miles away exercised any immediate and profound influence on the lives and habits of men in California who were fighting their own battles with a strange new environment. The business of national importance that most attracted their attention was the question of a railroad across the continent to the Pacific.

California sorely needed means for better communication with the East. The Overland

Mail, established in 1857, gave fairly reliable but none too speedy mail service. Transportation of goods was still far too slow and uncertain, despite the fact that the marvelous new clipper ships had cut in half the sailing time around the Horn. The Pony Express, established in 1860, was never of great economic importance, and the transcontinental stage lines that soon followed came too late and were quite inadequate to take care of the great number of emigrants bound for the Far West. In the first ten years of her life as a state, two hundred and fifty thousand immigrants came into California, and the majority of them followed the overland trails of their predecessors of '49. By the time the Civil War broke out, almost four hundred thousand Californians were clamoring for quicker communication with the East, and for better means of transportation.

It was the war that finally brought both of these wishes to fulfilment. Spurred on by military need, Congress passed the necessary legislation, and on July 1, 1862, President Lincoln signed the Pacific Railroad Bill, which also provided aid for the construction of a transcontinental telegraph line. The building of the Central Pacific Railroad in California, and its struggles with its eastern rival, the Union Pacific, form one of the most colorful and romantic chapters in the history of California, yet the great and lasting significance of the building of the railroad is rather to be found in its consequences.

For eight years after the incorporation of the Central Pacific Railroad Company of California, the builders labored to complete the great project. In the East, the rival Union Pacific company extended its lines toward the West, where desperate and determined workers built eastward from California. Then on the 10th of May, 1869, President Grant read the following telegram:

> "Sir, we have the honor to report that the last rail is laid, the last spike is driven. The Pacific Railroad is finished."

"Finished, too, for California," says Cleland, "was much that had made her previous history —slow going ox wagons no longer crossed the Sierras; the mining counties dwindled in population, while the agricultural regions and the cities took on increasing life; great land grants of early days were gradually broken up to make room for a rapidly enlarged population; the cattle baron retired to the foothills and out of the way valleys to make way for grain fields, orchards and vineyards; the San Joaquin and Sacramento Valleys began to fulfill the old prophecies that one day they would become the granary of the Pacific; California products made their appearance in eastern markets; and eastern tourists daily enriched the California merchants. Travel became a source of unity and culture; thousands of persons, long stranded on the coast because of the difficult overland journey, rushed eagerly back to their old homes in the States; and after a brief stay, rushed even more eagerly back to the west, tenfold more enthusiastic for California than ever they had been before. Real estate booms grew to be familiar phenomena; labor problems thrust themselves upon the public notice; and the state government failed more and more to meet the demands of its citizens; society and business became more complex. On every side new forces—social, economic, political—marked the development of a new day."

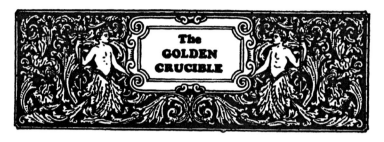

The GOLDEN CRUCIBLE

XI

FOR the generation that witnessed its completion, the railroad directly or indirectly caused almost as much evil as good. It did indeed mark the development of a new day, but a day that was ushered in by a stormy dawn. The decade of the seventies was a period of general unrest and discontent. The economic life of the State, though well on its way toward stability after the golden era of '49, was still far from its fullest development. Industry and agriculture were growing rapidly, but were still struggling under adverse circumstances. Much of the best land was held in virtual monopolies by private owners under old Mexican grants, by the railroad under Federal grants for financial aid in construction, and by corporations or speculators who by devious methods had obtained large holdings of State or Federal land. Business suffered from the after effects of the panic of 1873, and the depression lasted for a number of years. In this period of social and economic transition a rapidly growing population did not always find means for gaining a livelihood.

Besides these underlying economic factors a craze for speculation in shares of the Comstock Lode mines swept over the State in the seventies and seriously affected the lives and thoughts of the public as a whole. The public mind, says Eldredge, appeared to be demoralized. Responsibility sat lightly on the shoulders of those with power. Public officials and directors of mining and other corporations exploited their positions for their own private gain, all following "the good old rule of Rob Roy

'The simple plan
That they shall take who have the power
And they shall keep who can.' "

The railroad builders were great in natural power and intelligence, but their ethics were those of their time. They were direct, forceful, shrewd, unscrupulous, hard, and grasping, men who quite naturally followed "the simple plan." As soon as the main line of the Central Pacific was finished, they turned their attention toward consolidating their power in the State. They acquired railroad property that gave them control of all the traffic coming from east, north, or south of San Francisco Bay. They built into the San Joaquin Valley, and sent spurs from the main line west to shut off competition from the coast.* They beat the Eastern builders at their own game, and met every threat of outside competition by their organization within California. They established a monopoly that was still further strengthened in 1884 when the Southern Pacific Company was chartered—which "has since controlled the combined properties of the Central and Southern Pacific Railroad Companies." Besides this transportation monopoly, which was used to extort all that the traffic would bear, the railroad builders dominated local politics, where they ruled as the real power in the State.

Meanwhile, the public, restless and dissatisfied, seized upon these real and other fancied grievances, and demanded a new constitution to correct abuses that flourished under the old one. Cleland sums up their main causes for complaint: "corruption and inefficiency in gov-

---

*The Southern Pacific Railroad, which began as a competitor of the Central Pacific, never seriously threatened the latter's dominance. According to Cleland, the two roads had, to all intents and purposes, merged their interests by 1871. The "Big 4" of the C. P. bought the small California railroad known as the "S. P." They then used it in forestalling the Texas Pacific and putting an end to threats from that quarter by building the road on the southern route themselves. C. P. and S. P. were twin children of the Big 4.

ernment; the evils of the railroad situation, and the political activities of the Central Pacific; large land and water monopolies, accompanied by unfair methods of taxation; wages and conditions of labor; and finally, unrestricted immigration of Chinese coolies."

With these and other even more fundamental if less tangible sources of discontent vaguely realized by the public, it was natural that it should seek some sacrificial goat to be led to the altar of public condemnation. And the heathen Chinee was at hand to serve admirably for the purpose. The luckless Oriental objectified the fears and symbolized all the racial prejudices of a dissatisfied American populace. The Chinaman was an inferior being, but he was alien, foreign, strange, and therefore dangerous, evil, ominous. Away with him! "The Chinese must go!"

Eldredge says that Chinese immigration began in 1848, when three Chinese were brought into California—two men and one woman. Almost eight hundred had followed them by January, 1850, and the following August a group of the "China boys" were cheered by a friendly crowd as they marched in a San Francisco parade. A year or so later the Governor of the State spoke of them as "one of the most worthy classes of our newly adopted citizens" and advocated their increased immigration so that their labor might be used in reclaiming swamp and overflow lands, "to the economic gain of the state."

Time and further immigration changed all that. The Chinese had been disliked almost from the first wherever their industry and thrift had brought them into competition with white labor, as for example in the mines. Finally, by 1876, the presence of 116,000 Chinese in a total population of about 800,000 constituted a serious threat to the social and economic well-being of the State, though it can well be doubted that they were to any considerable extent responsible for all the economic evils charged against them. They were a conspicuous part of the economic complex, however, and when unrest and dissatisfaction had finally permeated the public consciousness it was inevitable that they should bear the brunt of popular fury. Agitation against them reached its climax in 1875, says Cleland, when "a sort of hysteria began to sweep over the state, and the phrase, 'The Chinese must go!' became the battle cry of a frenzied crusade."

The laboring class was the most vocal, and the most injured. They felt, with some reason, that they were being forced into competition with "Chinese cheap labor." Many Chinese had been imported by the railroad builders to augment the white labor that too often had proved unavailable or unreliable. The road was now completed, but many Chinese were still being retained as manual laborers. The white laboring population had grown in the meantime, and now that times were hard and jobs scarce, neither the Chinese nor the railroad was in very high favor with the laboring public or those who were in sympathy with it.

The time was ripe for a labor revolt, and it came. Fortunately the revolt was political rather than physical, though anti-Chinese riots took place in various parts of the State. An Irish teamster, haranguing crowds of disaffected workmen gathered on the sandy, vacant lots of San Francisco, succeeded in organizing them into a labor party known to local political history as the Workingmen's Party. The somewhat radical doctrines embodied in its platform became known collectively and sometimes scornfully as Kearneyism, from the name of the party's Irish founder.

Although membership in the Workingmen's Party was confined largely to the more radical or irresponsible part of the population, a number of sincere and brilliant men belonged to it, and public dissatisfaction was so general throughout the State that its program received considerable support in the Constitutional Convention of 1878. It was especially influential in bringing to a successful issue the problem of Chinese immigration, and in molding provisions designed to curb the activities of all kinds of monopolies—of land, water, trade and above all those of the railroad's corporate organizations. The Workingmen's Party, though internal dissension soon broke its ranks and destroyed its political effectiveness, marked the rise of labor as a new and henceforth vital factor in State life.

The new constitution adopted in 1879 could provide no effective means for the exclusion of the Chinese.* By this time, however, popular agitation against them had reached such a point that Congress gave heed. Within a few years Federal legislation was passed suspending their further immigration, and this particular yellow peril became a thing of the past. With other matters within the jurisdiction of the State, the

*This required Federal legislation.

new organic law dealt more successfully. For example, it provided for a more equitable system of taxation, for official regulation of the sale of water for irrigation, and, especially and hopefully, for methods to regulate the public service corporations in their relations with the public.

Of the latter, the railroad and its subsidiary corporate organizations came in for considerable attention. The new constitution provided for a State Board of Railroad Commissioners with powers deemed ample for the protection of the public against unfair practices. The general public fondly believed that the railroad's hold on the State's political and economic life would now be broken, but it took until the end of the century, and longer, before that hold was broken by the statewide reform movement following the San Francisco graft prosecutions of 1906. As late as 1897 the Mayor of San Francisco could write: "We have the suspected corruption of public bodies, legislators, and supervisors; and even courts are exposed to the machinations of the corporations, which, with the Southern Pacific Company, the overshadowing monopoly of the state, have been classified by the people in impotent wrath as the 'associated villainies.' They have debauched politics and established a government within a government, more powerful in normal times than the State Government itself."

As against this, Cleland quotes from a letter written about twenty years later by a prominent official of the Southern Pacific Company: "In time it became obvious to the managers of the Company that the disadvantages of these political activities so far outbalanced any possible benefits the Company would derive from them, that it became the policy to discontinue whatever political activities existed, and after 1893 it was the constant effort of the Company to divorce itself from its former relations to politics. This it had largely succeeded in doing prior to the time of Governor Johnson's election in 1910."*

*In a brief essay, such as this, one cannot hope to evaluate justly the many factors involved in the bitter controversy caused by the earlier tactics of the California railroad builders. There can be no doubt that the railroad hierarchy was often unfair and oppressive in its dealings with the public, but in view of the complexity of the whole problem, one can here attempt only to set down the opposing points of view, and hope that the interested reader will look further into history before arriving at a final conclusion .

The
GOLDEN
CRUCIBLE

XII

DESPITE the preoccupation of the public mind with politics, and despite the
fact that the new constitution fulfilled
a real and urgent need, neither of these things
was so important as the underlying social and
economic forces that called them forth. The
political activities of a people, however absorb-
ing to the Anglo-Saxon mind, are but the out-
ward expressions of deeper and less realized
forces. The social and economic current of
events is the stream of fundamental power, with
politics appearing more often as the froth upon
the surface, showing, perhaps, which way the
stream is tending, but with little power to control its course. Nowhere is this more likely to
be true than in the life of a frontier community.
The Constitution of 1879 represented the attempt of the people of California to devise a
new organ of government to fit the new set of
circumstances brought about by the changes of

the preceding thirty years. They were reasonably successful, but the passage of thirty more years would bring about further changes in their life that would lead to further changes in their organic law.

The thirty years that had elapsed since the days of '49 had indeed wrought a great change in the Californian scene. This change, however, was but the logical outgrowth of forces taking their origin at the time of the gold rush. The gold discovery was undoubtedly the most fateful accident in California's varied history. It came just as the Treaty of Guadalupe Hidalgo confirmed the sovereignty of the United States in California, and just in time to direct and accelerate the swelling tide of American emigration toward the Far West.

Others than the American emigrants felt the pull of the golden magnet. West of the Pacific and east of the Atlantic thousands responded to the lure. Gold has ever been a symbol to awaken man's hope for better fortune and arouse his lust for sudden gain. And California was gold.

Thus as a result of a workingman's chance discovery, two great streams of human energy converged within a small area in a new and almost unknown land. Here the energy of the expanding frontier met the energy released by the discovery of gold. California became a great golden crucible that held within its mountainous rims all the elements of a new kind of American life.

It had been the dream of ancient alchemists to transmute base metals into gold. The Californians of '49 had a harder task. They had to transmute gold into human values.

Part of the process by which this difficult transmutation took place has already been described. That process is not unique with California, for it is common to all human history. For the history of human society is the history of man's progressive struggle with his environment. Nowhere else is this struggle reproduced so graphically, or so typically, within such a small compass of time and space, as in California during the half-century between 1850 and 1900.

The California of 1850 provided an environment for the display of human energy that was quite new and in many respects unique. The individual set down in that new California was a unit of free energy, hardly yet capable of impressing itself on the strange environment, to say nothing of controlling it. In this unprecedented social situation all ties of custom and convention were broken. For a few short years man was nearly free of the incubus of the past. No ancestral dead lay in his graveyards. Almost he was free in the present. Old social restrictions had been removed: new ones had not yet been imposed. Old patterns of behavior had been broken up: new ones had not yet formed out of the surrounding confusion. In the mines, men were reduced to an essential equality, simply because they faced a situation that was new to all alike. Their common equality grew out of their common ignorance. Chance gave uncertain direction to their actions. Skill, like wisdom, would come only with time and patience. Even in San Francisco, where the commercial and political leaders of the State had the accumulated experience of the past to guide them, uncertainty, hazard, and chance characterized the life of the day.

Thirty years of intense activity had changed much of that old life and had brought much order out of that primary confusion. In three decades human energy had accomplished much. Now a new generation was at hand to receive the heritage left by its predecessors, to estimate the quality and the value of the life that had grown out of '49, and to carry on as best it might with the eternal process.

Despite the great progress that had been made, California was still a society in process of formation. It would require the labors of this second generation to complete the task of State building. Yet these Californians of 1880 were not a generation that had grown up with the State. Not one in five of them had been living in California in 1850. Only a few of them had been born in the State. This is amusingly illustrated by the following anecdote: In the year that marked the completion of the Pacific railroad, "a fine old pioneer . . . had an idea. He would organize the native sons of California. . . They met, those native sons of 1869. They responded numerously and enthusiastically to the general's call. But the general was dismayed. The native sons of California in 1869 were for the most part little boys in knee pants."

There were not many more native sons ten years later. More than a third of the total number of inhabitants in 1880 had come into California in the decade immediately preceding. And of the more than eight hundred and fifty thousand people then in the State, over one-third of them had come from foreign lands. At that time there were thirty-four foreigners in every one hundred Californians. Of these thirty-four, there were about nine Chinese (three of the nine lived in or near San Francisco), seven Irish, five German, three English, two Canadian, and one French. The remaining seven were of various other nationalities.

Here was one reason for the tolerant individualism that was so characteristic of early society in California. With all these men and women of different origins, different national ideals, different traditions, and different outlooks, it is not surprising that Californian life should have have been so free of the narrow restrictions of a less cosmopolitan society. These men of different race and creed lived for the most part in harmony. The process of time, the rapid growth of a not yet large population, and the growing demands of an increasingly complex environment had taught them to work together, though for many years to come their life would retain the hallmark of an individualism that was one of California's proudest boasts.

The growing economic importance of the State was evidence of their industry and genius for hard work. By 1880 they had improved ten million acres of farm land as compared with six million in 1870. Two million acres of these ten were planted to wheat, two-thirds of a million to hay, and half a million to barley. These three farm crops together produced to the value of fifty-seven million dollars in that one year, more than double the figures for the same crops in 1870.

Almost thirty-six thousand farms dotted the arable areas of the State, where hardly twenty-four thousand could have been found ten years earlier. There were still many large land holdings, but the land was steadily and more equitably being divided among small land holders. By the end of the century most of the large grain ranches had been broken up to provide opportunities for the more intensive cultivation of specialized crops. Completing the process, dairies and orchards and vineyards took their place with the smaller farms to provide the diversification of products that makes for a sound agricultural economy.

In the towns, beside the growing value of the various forms of trade, industry was beginning to threaten the economic lead of agriculture, just as agriculture earlier had threatened the supremacy of gold. In this same year of 1880, forty-three thousand industrial workers in fifty-eight hundred establishments produced manufactured goods worth one hundred and fifteen million dollars. These figures were to increase rapidly. By 1904 the annual value of manufactures was more than three hundred and sixty-seven million dollars.

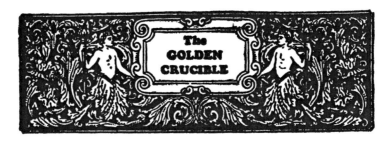

XIII

OBVIOUSLY, much had been done to build up the new State: but the whole had not yet been formed from all the parts. The quarter century following 1880 saw that task completed, when Southern California at last came into its own. In 1880, however, Southern California was still an isolated section of the State. Los Angeles was hardly more than a primitive Mexican pueblo, where an odd mixture of old American settlers, hard headed Yankees, and prosaic European merchants lived in peaceful accord with the social remnant of the old California culture that still persisted in a few of the older settlements—Monterey, Santa Barbara, Los Angeles, San Diego.

Their life was quiet and primitive. They had not yet met the challenge of their northern neighbors. San Francisco as late as 1880 held one-fourth of the State's population and most of its working capital. The eleven thousand inhabitants of its future rival, Los Angeles, were still placidly engaged in the ordinary routine of trade. In the outlying districts, a few new settlers shared the land with old-timers ranching in the shadow of the foothills. Further south, a mere handful of people—about twenty-five hundred —lived on the shores of San Diego's land-locked bay, and hoped for the time when a railroad would connect them with the outside world.

Southern California's day of isolation was soon ended. Two things combined to draw it to a close, the same two things which were to cause the great real estate boom of 1887—publicity and the railroad. The name of California, of course, was already known throughout the world, but its fame rested on the gold of '49. Now the Californians of a later generation advertised their land, their climate, and their romance. Snowbound New England read of California's perpetual sunshine. The Middle West heard of a land that instead of—or rather, in addition to—wheat and corn, would grow the exotic fruits of other lands. From Maine to Texas, old and young read the romantic story of Ramona, and other less popular but more lurid books of description.

A new sort of emigration was ready to leave

for California. The old, the tired, the ill, and the discouraged, as well as the young, the restless, and the ambitious, were all eager to try their fortunes in the new California, "where the flowers catch fire with beauty; among the orange groves; beside the olive trees; where the pomegranates wear calyx crowns; where the figs of Smyrna are turning; where the bananas of Honolulu are blossoming; where the chestnuts of Italy are dropping; where Sicilian lemons are ripening," as one impassioned publicist found courage to write in the late seventies.

Then, in 1885, the Santa Fe railroad reached Los Angeles. Within two years the "Great Boom" was on. It was Southern California's first big real estate boom. Professional "boomers" came in from the Middle West and added more than their share to the general excitement and speculative mania. Land skyrocketed in price. It was sold and resold, divided and subdivided. And then the bottom fell out.

Disillusioned, but not disheartened, the people of Southern California, who by 1890 numbered three times as many as in 1880, settled down to the hard and sustained labor that so soon was to show a rich return. Although boosters had exaggerated the immediate possibilities of the new country, their exaggerations were based on fundamental realities. For the value was there in the land, the sun did shine— almost perpetually—and fruits and flowers did grow, almost as luxuriantly as had been promised.

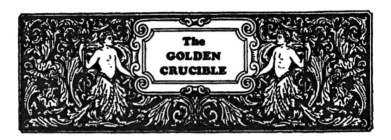

The
GOLDEN
CRUCIBLE

XIV

MEANWHILE other parts of the State had been developing steadily. The close of the century at last brought California near to fulfillment of the promise inherent in those wild, chaotic days of the gold rush. California was still a new state, but one far removed from the pioneer community which gave it birth. A complex civilization had grown up in the land that but a half-century earlier had provided only for the simple needs of a pastoral people, or for the even simpler needs of Indian aborigines. Filaments of iron and steel had entered the social fabric which in earlier days had been shot through with the gleam of virgin gold. Life as a whole flowed in more ordered patterns of behavior imposed by the necessities of a new order of things.

Lines of social and economic coördination bound the State from one end to the other. Railroads crossed its length and breadth, tying together the various sections into an economic whole. North and south, east and west, the physical environment was gradually yielding to the pressure of man's directed energy. California began to give up for human use and need still more of its natural resources. Timber from the northern coast and the Sierra was cut and manufactured for the manifold uses of society. Water from mountain rivers was diverted for use in reclaiming land hitherto thought worthless, or to turn the turbines that would change its elemental energy into electric power. In the south, gold flowed black, and the oil industry was beginning a cycle of development that was to affect the general community almost as profoundly as had mining, two generations earlier. Thus the products of one section complemented those of another, to provide a diversification of interests that furthered the economic stability of a society which already had attained social order.

So California at the turn of the century was prepared for a new age in both its own and the nation's life. The State had developed an essential unity, and could now take its rightful place as an integral part of the whole nation. It was well that this was so, for California in 1900 faced a new period in American life, wherein the United States would achieve a new kind of union, one in which the motion picture, the newspaper, and the machine would replace the frontiersman's rifle and the engineer's transit as agencies of national development.

California was ready for this new age. The State was organized as a whole. It was prepared to welcome and assimilate the two million new-comers who in the first two decades after 1900 were to double its population and its wealth. California and the Californians were ready for this new period in their life, but they could not have been quite aware of its imminence. For there is no record that they gave heed to the departure from San Francisco, in the spring of 1903, of the first automobile to complete a trans-continental journey across the United States. It was a messenger from the new West, a herald of the new age.

ADDENDA
SOCIAL AND INTELLECTUAL LIFE
OF CALIFORNIA: 1850-1906
By BLAKE ROSS

It is probable that histories can be written in as many ways as there are historians to write them. Faced with an appalling number of uncoordinated historical data, the historian must exercise his individual judgment in discriminating between them, in order to select those items which appear most significant in the general plan of his work. The necessity for selection, however, leads inevitably to omission. Since, in writing The Golden Crucible, I chose to devote myself to a presentation of the general structure of events in the historical process, it became necessary to omit virtually all discussion of the more human aspects of State life. The purpose of this final note is to remedy this omission by a brief discussion of Californian life and cultural achievements during the first half century of Statehood.

Well, then, what of the Californian himself, and what of the more human aspects of Californian life in the period covered by this essay? What of the habits and beliefs of the Californians? What of their artists and writers? What of the typically Californian way of life which developed coincidentally with the more impersonal processes of State growth?

One hesitates before answering. What, precisely, do we mean by the adjective "Californian," which we use so often and with such assurance? What are the characteristics and attributes which make a thing "typically" Californian?

Happily, this is not the place to attempt an extended answer to such questions, even though we find them implied every time we speak of Californian culture. That there was a certain special kind of culture growing out of the early Californian life is a fact which can easily be shown, though it is not so easy to indicate in what respects it was unique in California.

This difficulty results from the confusion of the native with the alien elements of her culture. A stable and homogeneous society develops a culture which usually reveals certain definite characteristics, peculiar to itself. It develops traditions which serve in part to distinguish it from other societies. Its arts, flowering in a society which has persisted long enough to establish cultural stability and social homogeneity, serve further to indicate the characteristic quality of its civilization. But Californian society was certainly far from stable during those early years of rapid change, and it has never become really homogeneous. California has historical traditions, but her traditions, when they come from the outside, are various and derivative, and when they are authentically her own, they are traditions of action rather than of creative thought or esthetic feeling. Hence the confusion of cultural elements which makes it so difficult to define the essentially Californian traits of Californian life, art, and literature.

Old American traditions and novel problems of life were the chief social forces at work in the new California and were also the chief sources of social change or conflict. The miners and early pioneers brought with them the ideals and traditions of their original homes, and retained them intact or modified them according to the exigencies of the new Californian environment.

It appears that religion, for example, remained essentially unchanged, though religious services in the more primitive communities were marked by the pleasing informality that was one of the outstanding characteristics of early Californian life. Fundamental religious beliefs underwent no marked change, and from the days of '49 on to the present the Catholic Church and the various Protestant sects have been faithfully carrying on their traditional work with erring humanity—which on the whole has been not much more errant in California than elsewhere.

Although fundamental beliefs were little disturbed by their transfers from older and more settled communities to the uncertain conditions of the new land, it is not surprising to find that many common social customs and moral habits, usually associated with traditional religious beliefs, underwent a change. It has already been suggested in the main body of the essay that the more masculine diversions, such as drinking and gambling, were generally recognized by society at large as defensible if not strictly commendable.

In addition to such peccadillos, one finds further evidence of the lessened influence of religious beliefs on behavior. Hubert Howe Bancroft notes that from the outset, "Sunday became identified with enjoyment rather than with solemn devotion. The voyage out (from the East) had sufficed to break down puritanical habits." Even with the passage of time and the establishment of a more decorous social order, attempts to impose a stricter observance of religious conventions were successfully resisted. "The several efforts made since the early fifties to secure the religious observance of the Sabbath have not been very successful in the large towns, and Sunday is practically Germanized. Multitudes then pour out to bask in the sunlit valleys of the surrounding bay shore, or to promenade to the music at the park, watching at the same time the throng of carriages on the way to the ocean beach."

Religion, in short, was affected by the dominant individualism of the times, and by the seductive charms of the Californian climate and scenery. These two elements in State life, the one social and the other physical, are indeed the two things that stand out with any clearness as being essentially Californian. At least, they exerted a powerful and pervasive influence on the Californians and their actions. One finds direct and indirect evidence in almost every phase of social life.

Josiah Royce, himself a native Californian, asserts the belief that the nature and climate of the Californian environment exert a marked influence upon the Californian. A native of California, he thinks, feels a peculiarly intimate relationship with nature. The mildness of the climate takes him often into the open country. He sees the characteristic landscape in a clear and sunny light, and he becomes accustomed to long vistas and sharp outlines. Above all, he senses the "fundamental rhythm" of the seasons, in which the annual coming of the rains is an event of profound significance, corresponding in some respects to the coming of Spring in other regions. A certain change in one's personality results from this intimacy with nature. "You get a sense of power from these wide views, a habit of personal independence from the contemplation of a world which the eye seems to own."

Aside from such psychological consequences, the Californian environment has other effects upon social and individual life. The beneficence of nature and the relative regularity of the weather make the Californian less subject to the hardship and uncertainty of life under more severe conditions. This makes social life freer and easier, and encourages the informal hospitality so widely found in earlier days. It leads to independence in speech and action. It also lends itself to either virtue or vice, for nature, benevolently neutral, lends herself with equal indifference to idleness, moral carelessness, or hard work.

All these characteristics of climate and natural environment fostered the growth of that independence and individuality which at first were developed by the hardships experienced by the miner and the pioneer. It is difficult to trace cause and effect in this relationship, for one finds the influence of the environment inextricably entangled in the web of tradition which grew out of American pioneer life, the political ideals of Jacksonian Democracy, the Spanish tradition in California, and life in the Californian mining era. Whatever it may have resulted from, however, a definite and dominant individualism was characteristic of early Californian life.

We have seen how that individualism affected religious habits of life. Its effects also could have been observed in the political independence of the early Californians, as well as in practically all forms of social and business life. Men were judged upon their own merits. Questions of caste and ancestry carried no weight. Independence of thought and action was characteristic of life in general.

The geographical isolation of California also fostered the kind of healthy provincialism described by Royce in his essay on "Provincialism." The better kind of provincialism is not narrowly selfish nor intolerant of outside opinion, but will have a tendency to conserve its own local customs and ideals, and to foster pride and self-respect in the individual who identifies himself with his own community. This sort of provincialism is a social force which opposes the leveling tendency of the times, and therefore preserves social variety, individuality, and a sense of personal responsibility.

It is true that a certain kind of social irresponsibility was frequently found associated with Californian individualism. This, however, was more likely to be true of political and civic life in general, for in his private life the Californian had a marked sense of personal responsibility.

In reviewing the development of Californian literature, one finds the same difficulty in separating the native elements from those derived from alien sources and old traditions that he found in attempting an analysis of other Californian activities. Yet here the task is somewhat easier, for if the reviewer disregard the great mass of local writing on the grounds that it is a hopelessly hybrid mixture of foreign and derivative material, he will discover a vein which may justly be characterized as Californian.

Bret Harte contributed to literature several characterizations which were about as "typically" Californian as may be. Jack Hamlin was "the" Californian gambler, and Yuba Bill "the" Californian stage-coach driver. Colonel Starbottle, caricature though he was, personified certain unmistakable characteristics of the Southern Gentlemen as he was known to Californians. The Heathen Chinee transcended his lowly origin and became an authentic figure in the Californian pantheon. There were similar semi-legendary heroes in all the folklore of the West, of course, but Harte's genius fixed the Californian type in the minds of readers all over the world.

Bret Harte was not the first who felt the stimulus and who accepted the opportunities of the new Californian life, nor is his humor the first to find written expression. It was an army officer, sent to California before it was a state, who first made notable contribution to the Californian literature of humor. Captain George H. Derby, better known under his pen name "John Phoenix," found in the Californian environment an opportunity for the expression of that kind of humor which has come to be known, in its wider aspects, as peculiarly American. In fact, it may be said that the school of American humor first came into being in California, for though it may have been developing at the same time in other parts of the nation, its definitely characteristic expression was first manifested in the early Californian environment. Mark Twain himself, the dean of American humorists, spent several formative years in Nevada and California, which at that time constituted one cultural area.*

In the latter half of the century there were several other writers whose work may justly be described, in part or in whole, as Californian. Josiah Royce, though most of his reputation was made in the East, was born and bred a Californian, and was a graduate of the University of California. Ambrose Bierce should also be included in this list. Although he was not a native Californian, he lived for the latter half of his life in the vicinity of San Francisco, where he enlivened the columns of the old Wasp, the Argonaut, and the Examiner, with caustic comments on life and manners in California and the nation.

There are many others who might be mentioned, but one must draw the line somewhere. The "Progress and Poverty" of Henry George, published in 1879, still commands the interest of students of the social sciences. At the turn of the century, the young Californian novelist, Frank Norris, attracted the attention of the nation with his powerful novels. Two of his best known, "McTeague" and "The Octopus," deal with Californian material. Jack London is too well known to require further comment, as also is Gertrude Atherton, who is a native Californian and whose stories and novels often deal with Californian scenes and characters. The poet, George Sterling, likewise, is a Californian writer who is remembered with affection and esteem.

This brief review cannot hope to mention all Californian writers by name. The reader is referred to the "Story of the Files" and "Literary California," by Ella Sterling Cummins (Mighels), which reveal the fascinating variety and astonishing abundance of earlier Californian writing, and will serve admirably as a point of departure for further research.

Californian poetry presents the same difficulty of definition which was mentioned at the beginning of this review.

---

*For valuable information on Bret Harte's work and Californian humor, I am indebted to Professor George R. Stewart of the University of California, whose biography of Bret Harte, now in preparation, should provide a notable contribution to Californiana.

In discussing a form of esthetic expression so complex and personal as poetry, one finds it more difficult than ever to pick out elements which could fairly be considered as being essentially Californian. Even though poetry be an expression of the sensitive individual mind, it is greatly dependent upon tradition for its form and vocabulary, and that dependence upon tradition must inevitably determine much of what the poet has to say, whether he will it or not. In this respect, Californian poets of the early period seem to have followed tradition, and to have made few original contributions of note.

Leaving these general considerations aside, however, it is obvious that the poet will be affected by the environment in which he lives. Some of the poems of Joaquin Miller and Ina Coolbrith—to mention two of the best known—reveal such influence. And, if one wishes to speak simply of poetry, without trying to qualify it as Californian, there are many others whose verse might be included.

The question of definition arises again to balk criticical discussion of the arts of painting, sculpture, and architecture, but here the problem is greatly simplified by virtue of the fact that there was little original art created in the formative period of the State. There was too much work to be done, and too much social confusion, to allow full play of esthetic genius.

Bruce Porter recognizes this in his charming and sympathetic essay on "Art and Architecture in California." "The arts with which we deal here, require for their orderly growth and flowering, a quiet unattainable in a new and lusty civilization . . . . Speech and writing travel with so easy and light an equipment, they can foot it with the pioneers; the graphic and monumental arts must delay until the hearths are established and the time has come to build the temple. They move with the encumbrance of a tradition, they require the serenities of a civilization established and the response assured." Nevertheless, "the absence of art does not of necessity indicate an absence of a widespread (though unconscious) appreciation of beauty."

And here let us leave the vexatious question of Californian art and literature, secure in the conviction that the early Californians established the hearth around which we or our descendants may build the temple, and humble in the knowledge that when great art comes to our shores it will partake of the universal and transcend the narrow limits of provincial labor.

The real greatness of our Californian ancestors lay in the work they did, not in their thought or art. It is no small task to build, in two short generations, the social and economic structure of a state like California, where the very richness and variety of its natural resources were at once a challenge and an inspiration to men who came from all corners of the world, hopeful of fortune but untaught by precedent from the life to which they had been accustomed.

Some idea of the nature and complexities of their larger problems has been given in the main essay, and some idea also of the ways in which those problems were met. Yet that is not the whole story. In the midst of their labors, the Californians found time for the ordinary social activities of mankind. They found lusty enjoyment in their lives, and sometimes, failure and defeat. They loved, married, begot, and died. They drank and gambled, fought their battles, loved their women, hung men when occasion demanded, and sent their children to Sunday School, likewise when occasion demanded. They built saloons and churches, fine theatres and fine schools, transcontinental railroads and palatial homes. They burrowed in the earth, and found flight in poetry and prose.

In all this kaleidoscopic picture of the past, one sees growing out of confusion a life which in many ways exhibited a set of characteristics which we describe as Californian. The lines of definition are obscure and indeterminate, but somehow a sense of the whole prevails, and one feels that the first two generations of Californians produced something distinctive in American life. Somehow one feels a sense of spaciousness in their life, something which transcends the petty struggles for individual gain. It is associated with great spaces and wide horizons, and finds expression in human individuality and personal independence.

That distinctive life developed in the years following the gold rush, when the Californians came to the realization that in their new land they were participating in a life quite different from life elsewhere, and that this life could not be understood or felt by those outside the Californian borders. So it happened that "a definite local tradition of California life was developed upon the basis of the memories and characters that had been formed in the early days."

This tradition promised well until in 1869 the completion of the transcontinental railroad brought intrusive alien influences into the life of the State. A new immigration brought different ideas and different habits of life, and although it stubbornly resisted the onslaught of change, the old Californian spirit gave way before the steady pressure of these new social and economic forces. Slowly but inevitably the character of Californian life was transformed in the course of this struggle between the new and the old. Even in the California of today that subtle conflict still continues, unacknowledged and for the most part unrecognized, but promising to eradicate still further the distinguishing marks of the old Californian way of life.

How much of that old life still persists is a question for thoughtful consideration. Reluctantly one faces the conclusion that many of the old values have been lost in the process of time. What salvage we may find in the present is something to hold fast, and to perpetuate as best we may.

Yet change is no more than the manifestation of historical necessity. Times change, and with them, ourselves. Though our Californian life of today has lost some of the old values, it has gained new ones. We are no longer bounded by the desert and the Sierra on the east, nor by the long line of surf upon our western shore. We have, for better or for worse, merged our life with the life of the Nation. Our outlook, through the Golden Gate, spans the Pacific, and we, like our pioneer ancestors, turn our eyes once more toward the West.

ACKNOWLEDGMENT

Readers of Californiana will know that material for this essay has been gathered from the works of men who have contributed greatly toward a better knowledge of California's history. Owing to the circumstances under which this essay was written, it has been necessary to depend largely upon the works of such men. With the exception of a few magazine and newspaper articles, and several of the annual reports of the California State Board of Agriculture, it has been impossible to deal directly with source material.

The writer wishes to acknowledge his especial dependence upon the works of Josiah Royce, Zoeth Skinner Eldredge, Professor R. G. Cleland. Much of the material and many of his ideas have been appropriated from them.

Owing to the popular nature of this essay, footnotes and detailed references have been avoided, but are available for any possible future use. Besides several volumes on general American history, books and papers consulted in the preparation of this essay include:

CALIFORNIA: AN INTIMATE HISTORY—Gertrude Atherton.

ANNUAL REPORTS, 1911, 1912, 1913: California State Board of Agriculture.

CALIFORNIA: THE AMERICAN PERIOD—R. G. Cleland.

HISTORY OF CALIFORNIA—Z. S. Eldredge.

CALIFORNIA AND THE NATION: 1850-1869—Joseph Ellison.

HISTORY OF CALIFORNIA—T. H. Hittell.

IN AND OUT OF THE OLD MISSIONS—G. W. James.

RECOLLECTIONS OF A NEWSPAPER MAN—F. A. Leach.

SIXTY YEARS IN SOUTHERN CALIFORNIA—
Harris Newmark.

THE STORY OF CALIFORNIA—H. K. Norton.

ADDRESSES, REMINISCENCES, ETC., OF GENERAL JOHN BIDWELL—C. C. Royce.

CALIFORNIA—Josiah Royce.

STORY OF THE MINE—C. H. Shinn.

THE FORTY-NINERS—S. E. White.

CPSIA information can be obtained at www.ICGtesting.com
Printed in the USA
BVOW03s1100020215

385990BV00001B/41/P